stress

HUMAN BEHAVIOR

stress

BY OGDEN TANNER

AND THE EDITORS OF TIME-LIFE BOOKS

TIME-LIFE BOOKS, NEW YORK

The Author: Ogden Tanner, formerly an editor for
TIME-LIFE Books, is a freelance author whose most
recent book is the *Urban Wilds* volume of The
American Wilderness series. He was a feature writer
for the *San Francisco Chronicle* and an editor of
Architectural Forum. A native New Yorker, Mr.
Tanner and his family live in Connecticut.

General Consultants for Human Behavior:
Robert M. Krauss is Professor of Psychology at
Columbia University. He has taught at Princeton
and Harvard and was Chairman of the Psychology
Department at Rutgers. He is the co-author of
Theories in Social Psychology, edits the *Journal of
Experimental Social Psychology* and contributes
articles to many journals on aspects of human
behavior and social interaction.

Peter I. Rose is Sophia Smith Professor of Sociology
and Anthropology, and Director of the American
Studies Diploma Program at Smith College. He is
also a member of the graduate faculty of the
University of Massachusetts. His books include *They
and We, The Subject Is Race, The Study of Society,*
and *Sociology: Inquiring into Society.* Professor
Rose has also taught at Goucher, Wesleyan,
Colorado, Clark and Yale, and he has been a
Fulbright lecturer in England, Japan and Australia.

James W. Fernandez is Professor of Anthropology
at Princeton University. His research in culture
change has taken him to East, West and South
Africa and the Iberian peninsula. Articles and
monographs on his field studies have been widely
published in European and American anthropology
journals. He has been president of the Northeastern
Anthropological Association and a consultant to the
Foreign Service Institute. He taught previously at
Dartmouth College.

Special Consultant for Stress:
Jerome E. Singer is Professor of Psychology and
Sociology at the State University of New York at
Stony Brook. He served as Executive Secretary of a
committee of the National Academy of Sciences
established to study the social consequences of noise
abatement in transportation. Professor Singer is also
co-author of the book *Urban Stress.*

TIME-LIFE BOOKS

FOUNDER: Henry R. Luce 1898-1967

Editor-in-Chief: Hedley Donovan
Chairman of the Board: Andrew Heiskell
President: James R. Shepley

Vice Chairman: Roy E. Larsen

MANAGING EDITOR: Jerry Korn
Assistant Managing Editors: Ezra Bowen,
David Maness, Martin Mann, A. B. C. Whipple
Planning Director: Oliver E. Allen
Art Director: Sheldon Cotler
Chief of Research: Beatrice T. Dobie
Director of Photography: Melvin L. Scott
Senior Text Editors: Diana Hirsh, William Frankel
Assistant Planning Director: Carlotta Kerwin
Assistant Art Director: Arnold C. Holeywell
Assistant Chief of Research: Myra Mangan

PUBLISHER: Joan D. Manley
General Manager: John D. McSweeney
Business Manager: John Steven Maxwell
Sales Director: Carl G. Jaeger
Promotion Director: Paul R. Stewart
Public Relations Director: Nicholas Benton

HUMAN BEHAVIOR
Editorial Staff for *Stress:*
Editor: William K. Goolrick
Picture Editor: Kathy Ann Ritchell
Designer: John Martinez
Assistant Designer: Marion Flynn
Staff Writers: Richard Cravens, John Man,
Suzanne Seixas
Chief Researcher: Barbara Ensrud
Researchers: Oscar C. K. Chiang, Jane Sugden,
Dunstan Harris, Shirley Miller, Gail Nussbaum,
Constance R. Roosevelt, Ginger Seippel

Editorial Production
Production Editor: Douglas B. Graham
Assistant Production Editors: Gennaro C. Esposito,
Feliciano Madrid
Quality Director: Robert L. Young
Assistant Quality Director: James J. Cox
Associate: Serafino J. Cambareri
Copy Staff: Eleanore W. Karsten (chief),
Susan B. Galloway, Georgia Ingersoll,
Florence Keith, Pearl Sverdlin
Picture Department: Dolores A. Littles,
Jessy Faubert
Traffic: Carmen McLellan

Valuable assistance was given by the following departments and individuals of Time Inc.:
Editorial Production, Norman Airey; Library, Benjamin Lightman; Picture Collection,
Doris O'Neil; Photographic Laboratory, George Karas; TIME-LIFE News Service,
Murray J. Gart; Correspondents Margot Hapgood and Dorothy Bacon (London),
Ann Natanson and Deborah Sgardello (Rome), Maria Vincenza Aloisi and Josephine du Brusle
(Paris), Elisabeth Kraemer and Franz Spelman (Bonn), S. Chang (Tokyo), Leny Heinen
(Limburg), Mary Johnson (Stockholm), Traudl Lessing (Vienna), Bernard Diederich
(Mexico City), Bing Wong (Hong Kong).

Contents

That Keyed-up Feeling

1

For one of the couple at left a ride on a roller coaster is sheer delight —an exhilarating experience to be sought and savored for its own sake. For the other, clearly, it is an experience that almost brings panic. At the end of the ride, the man might very well say, "That was fun. Let's do it again someday." The woman might reply, "No, never. Once was enough for a lifetime!"

So far the situation seems ordinary enough. Two different people have had different emotional and behavioral responses to the same stressful experience of noise and swooping speed. What is not obvious is that, in one respect, they have had much the same response. Certain reactions inside their bodies have been almost identical. The ride, whether it was intensely enjoyable or intensely unpleasant, led to a characteristic pattern of physical changes. In both persons their hearts raced and pounded, and their blood pressures soared. A flood of hormones stimulated some organs and depressed the activity of others. Their breathing quickened, and their muscles tensed. These are the body's basic physiological reactions to stress. Other automatic reactions may vary, but these are always essentially the same, whatever the stress—good or bad, welcome or unwelcome.

To a scientist, stress is any action or situation that places special physical or psychological demands upon a person—anything that can unbalance his individual equilibrium. And while the physiological response to such demands is surprisingly uniform, the forms of stress are innumerable. A divorce is stressful—but so is a marriage. Getting fired is stressful—but so is getting a promotion. Stress may even be all but unconscious, like the noise of a city or the daily chore of driving a car. Perhaps the one incontestable statement that can be made about stress is that it belongs to everyone—to businessmen and professors, to mothers and their children, to factory workers, garbagemen and writers. A keyed-up feeling is part of the fabric of life.

Today, widely accepted ideas about stress are challenged by new research, and conclusions once firmly established may be turned completely around. The latest evidence suggests:

☐ Some stress is necessary to well-being, and a lack can be harmful.

☐ Stress may not be as much a factor in heart disease as many think (the debate continues).

☐ Stress definitely causes some serious ailments.

☐ Severe stress makes people accident-prone.

☐ Modern city stresses cause no more harm than old-fashioned country ones (the stresses are different, though).

☐ Disastrous stress on a group often has beneficial aftereffects.

Most people concern themselves mainly with the darker side of stress, as though stress were synonymous with distress. Certainly, negative stress is omnipresent. It may be as trivial as a jangling telephone or a slamming door that breaks concentration, as frightening as a fretful hornet at a picnic, as terrifying as a tipping kettle about to scald a child. It can be seen in the fuming commuter caught in a traffic jam; in the housewife fighting shopping crowds; in the university student confronting loneliness or a difficult examination. On a deeper level, it can be seen in the couple whose marriage is falling apart; in the family facing a separation or serious illness.

But the positive kind of stress is omnipresent too. It is reflected in the eyes and muscles of the Olympic skier in the starting gate or the champion runner in the blocks, the athlete who has psyched himself up for competition, yet keeps his tension under fine control to make it reward him with a burst of sustained effort. It can be seen too in the creative artist or composer seeking inspiration; in the singer giving a performance that brings down the house. Indeed, without stress not much would get done in this world. Any physical or mental effort, any problem-solving or decision-making, requires it to one degree or another, and it is through the stretching influence of stress that people and communities find unexpected resources within themselves and develop the capacity to meet new challenges.

In studying the effects of all stress, good and bad, scientists have worked in a number of distinct but interrelated areas. They have examined the everyday stresses of modern life, particularly the daily life of the large cities in which most of the world's industrialized peoples now live and work. To contrast with the stress of routine, they have studied episodes of high stress—the great turning points or crises in the lives of individuals and communities. They have attempted to measure both the temporary and the permanent effects of stress upon the human body. And they have sought practical ways of coping with stress, of avoiding or minimizing its negative effects and exploiting its good ones.

All of these studies are based upon examination of the three types of response to stress seen in the roller-coaster riders: emotional, behavioral and physiological, each distinguishable from but related to the others. The most obvious is the emotional response, ranging from mild annoyance to overpowering rage or fear, from amusement to ecstasy. For many people the emotional response is the only meaningful one —anything that bothers or elates them is stressful, and that is all there is to it—but emotions are difficult to measure.

Easier to analyze objectively is the second type of stress response: a change in performance or behavior, particularly as seen in certain actions that lend themselves to measurement. The effect of stress can be gauged by changes in the rate of error in carrying out a task, in productivity on the job or simply in the ability to get along with people. Stress in moderate doses will usually improve performance: an athlete subjects himself to the stresses of training to improve his strength and skill, a timid salesman forces himself to seek out customers. Yet even positive stress can impair performance: the error rate of someone about to marry usually rises during the week or two before the ceremony.

But it is the third type of response to stress, a physiological change or sequence of changes, that may have the deepest significance. These changes may go no further than such physical expressions of emotion as tears, but they also may so alter body functioning that, some scientists assert, they can lead to disease. According to specialists in the study of psychosomatic medicine—psychologically induced physical illness —stress can be a contributing factor in headaches, backaches, ulcers and heart disease.

Although there are three types of stress response, it is the third —the physiological reactions—that scientists have scrutinized most closely. The evidence has been there for everyone to see since the beginning of man's study of man. Most of these obvious reactions to stress are variable. Some people have always paled with fear, reddened with rage, blushed with embarrassment, retched in revulsion, wept in joy and sorrow, laughed out of pleasure, sympathy or cruelty. Under extreme stress, they have gone mad with mysterious passions or pined away from maladies with no apparent organic cause. Early societies ascribed such phenomena to demons that had taken possession of the body. In the Fourth Century B.C. the Greek philosopher Plato ventured the suggestion that "all diseases of the body proceed from the mind or soul."

In 1831 during the Industrial Revolution, a London physician named

James Johnson came closer. He characterized his city as a modern Babylon, where the "chafing tide of human existence" gave rise to ever-mounting tensions. These tensions, he argued, caused a condition of "body and mind intermediate between that of sickness and health, but much nearer to the former." Johnson called this condition the wear-and-tear complaint and suggested that it was a disease peculiar to the English, for whom business was almost the only pleasure, in contrast with the frivolous French, for whom pleasure was almost the only business. The most devastating effect of the disease, he observed, was the "careworn countenance" of premature old age.

In his approach to what would now be called psychosomatic medicine, Johnson went far beyond most of his contemporaries, who considered mind and body as separate entities. His description of the physical reaction to stress, in particular, was extraordinarily accurate for its day: "A sudden gust of passion, a transient sense of fear, an unexpected piece of intelligence—in short, any strong emotion of mind, will cause the heart to palpitate, the muscles to tremble, the digestive organs to suspend their functions, and the blood to rush in vague and irregular currents through the living machine." Johnson had spotted the signs of those universal stress reactions that, unlike tears or blushes, are not variable, but appear after every stress in every person.

Almost a century later, in the 1920s, the Harvard University physiologist Walter Cannon replaced Johnson's hunches and hints with the first scientific description of the basic automatic response to stress. In experiments with cats and dogs, Cannon proved that a complex animal body exhibits a single fundamental pattern of response to any challenge to its equilibrium. The response will vary in its force, depending on how important the challenge is perceived to be. But the response will always follow the same general pattern.

The challenge Cannon investigated was a severe one: danger. He theorized that an animal or a primitive man, faced by an enemy, will either prepare for combat or flee to safety; Cannon called this basic response to stress a fight-or-flight pattern. As refined later, this pattern embraces a train of changes in nerves and glands, a sequence that apparently is the innate result of eons of evolution.

This primal stress response begins in the very center of the brain, in the hypothalamus, a bundle of nerve cells that is no bigger than the tip of a thumb. It is a complex bundle; among its many functions are the regulation of growth, sex and reproduction. It also helps to stimulate such emotions as fear, rage and intense pleasure, which in some degree almost invariably accompany stress. In directing the basic physiological changes involved in stress, the hypothalamus acts in two ways. First, it controls the autonomic nervous system, which regulates the involuntary activities of the body's organs. Second, it activates the pituitary gland, which in turn orders the release of chemical messengers, or hormones, directly into the bloodstream. In some ways the two systems, nerves and hormones, reinforce each other to produce powerful, unmistakable signals; and yet they also balance and check each other to keep the body from running out of control. Taken together, they alter the functioning of almost every part of the body *(pages 16-17)*.

Many muscles of the body, to begin with, tense and tighten at the command of the automatic nerves. Through the action of some of these muscles, breathing becomes deeper and faster, the heart rate rises and blood vessels constrict, raising the blood pressure and almost completely closing the vessels just under the skin. The muscles of the face may contort in expressions of strong emotion; those of the nostrils and throat force these passages wide open. But other muscles suspend their function: the stomach and intestines temporarily halt digestion, while the muscles controlling the bowels and the bladder loosen. Elsewhere, the autonomic

Telltale reactions in the eye

Reactions of males and females to photographic subjects, as measured by eye-pupil opening or closing, are indicated by bars at each picture. The landscape turned women (white bar) off.

That people's eyes widen with fear, pleasure or other stresses is a common observation. However, when psychologist Eckhard Hess's wife remarked one evening that the pupils of his eyes changed size markedly as he scanned a book of photographs, Hess was inspired to try recording pupil opening and closing as a measure of emotional reaction. After testing hundreds of volunteers as they looked at photographs with varying emotional contents, he found a direct relationship: the greater the interest, the greater the dilation.

Hess's investigations also revealed characteristic patterns in the way men and women respond. Pictures like those below, which are taken from the book Hess wrote to describe his work, cause distinctly different reactions in the sexes—and one produces opposite reactions, causing men's pupils to open, but women's to close in a negative change revealing boredom.

PER CENT CHANGE IN PUPIL AREA

OPEN | CLOSE

30 20 10 0 −10

PER CENT CHANGE IN PUPIL AREA

CLOSE | OPEN

−10 0 10 20 30

nervous system calls for subtler but equally important changes: perspiration increases, while the secretion of saliva and mucus decreases. The sense organs sharpen perception; in the case of the eye, for example, physiologists discovered in the 1960s that pupils, which open and close to adjust vision to suit available light, dilate involuntarily during the stress response, even when the intensity of external light does not increase.

Finally, autonomic nerves directly stimulate the adrenal glands to release the hormones epinephrine and norepinephrine. These hormones generate the giddy exuberance mixed with anxiety that is felt "when the adrenalin is flowing"; some research suggests that epinephrine is particularly associated with fear, norepinephrine with rage. Their physiological influence is even more significant. They affect circulation, reinforcing the autonomic nervous system's action in elevating heartbeat and blood pressure. They signal the spleen to release more red blood corpuscles, they enable the blood to clot more quickly, and the bone marrow to produce more white corpuscles. The red blood cells carry oxygen that consumes food substances to produce energy; to give this oxygen more fuels to burn, the adrenals increase the amount of fat in the blood and stimulate the liver to produce more sugar.

While these actions are being set in motion by the adrenal glands, the pituitary too is reacting to signals from the hypothalamus. The pituitary secretes two hormones that play major roles in the basic stress response. One, the thyrotrophic hormone, or TTH, stimulates the thyroid, which increases the rate at which the body produces energy. The other, the adrenocorticotrophic hormone, or ACTH, reinforces the signals sent the adrenal glands through the autonomic nervous system. The ACTH hormone causes the outer layers of the adrenals to produce some 30 other hormones that are among the surest signs of stress; in laboratory experiments their concentration in the blood is often taken as a measure of its intensity.

All these signals, conveyed by nerve impulses and chemical surges, put the body in fighting trim, setting up behavior that is marvelously directed to meet a physical threat. Essentially, the body prepares for quick decisions, vigorous action and defense against injury. Hearing and smell become more acute and the dilation of eye pupils admits extra light for more sensitive seeing; in these ways vital information about the outer world is gathered. Faster breathing brings in more oxygen, and the mucous membranes of the nose and throat shrink to widen these passages for easier air flow. Within the body, the increased heart rate pumps extra blood with its richer loads of fuel and oxygen to the brain, lungs

Tieless, feet up, the very image of stress met and mastered, Hans Selye dictates into a microphone at a lap worktable of his own design in his office at Montreal's Institute of Experimental Medicine and Surgery. Under his direction, the Institute has become a leading center of stress research.

A relaxed explorer of stress

In 1926, a 19-year-old medical student, Hans Hugo Bruno Selye, was prompted to ask himself a simple-seeming question after an instructor had described the different symptoms of five diseases in five patients. Selye wanted to know what it meant just to be sick—not what distinguished one disease from another, but what linked them together, the symptoms that applied to all diseases and were the general nonspecific effects of illness. In exploring the meaning of "being sick," Selye established stress as a principal influence on all human behavior, whether in illness or in health.

In over a half century of laboratory research, conducted principally at the Institute of Experimental Medicine and Surgery of the University of Montreal, Hans Selye showed that almost any "assault"—fright, frustration, physical injury, infection—produced the same sequence of physiological changes within the body *(diagram, page 17)*. This sequence, called the General Adaptation Syndrome, was behind the observable effects associated with stress, and Selye attempted to identify it as a basic cause of all human ills.

Selye's later theories—among them the idea that everyone has an unreplenishable store of "adaptation energy" to combat stress—remain unproved. However, his work has provided some of the most significant of modern clues to the physical basis of human behavior.

and muscles; the resulting jump in energy production provides strength for fight or flight. But blood leaves the vessels near the skin, and its clotting time shortens, so that less blood will be lost if the body is wounded; a further precaution is the rapid proliferation of white blood cells, which counteract infection. Meanwhile, the skin perspires to flush out waste and cool the overheating system by evaporation. And the body conserves its store of energy for top-priority tasks when it temporarily shuts down activities that are not needed for fight or flight—digestion stops, the hunger-inducing flow of saliva slows and the bowels and bladder relax.

The significance of these almost instantaneous changes was explored and greatly extended by Hans Selye, the Vienna-born endocrinologist heading Montreal's Institute of Experimental Medicine and Surgery. Selye began his work as a medical student in Prague in 1936 and wrote the first book devoted exclusively to stress in 1950 (in a recent year, about 6,000 publications on the subject appeared). While Cannon worked with cats and dogs, Selye turned mainly to the most common of all experimental animals, the rat. He subjected his rats not only to extreme heat and cold, traumatic injury and chemical injections, but also to less severe stresses such as nervous irritation. He found, for example, that when the body and limbs of a naturally active rat are firmly held down, the animal exhibits clear symptoms of fear and rage, much like those associated with the fight-or-flight reaction.

From studies of these injured or immobilized rats, Selye worked out a detailed sequence of behavior that he proposed as the generally applicable aftermath of stress. This so-called general adaptation syndrome consists of a three-part pattern of responses over a period of time. The first part, an "alarm reaction," includes most of the automatic physiological activity isolated by Cannon and corresponds roughly to his fight-or-flight response. In the second part of the pattern, the "stage of resistance," the stressed animal's functions return to normal, and its resistance to further stimuli rises. If severe stress continues, the third and final "stage of exhaustion" may occur: the symptoms of the alarm reaction reappear, this time irreversibly, and the animal soon dies. According to Selye, it dies because it has exhausted its fund of "adaptation energy"—it has been unable to alter its behavior to accommodate the stress. And when the dead animal is dissected, it invariably has enlarged adrenal glands; shrunken lymphatic nodes and thymus (organs that play a vital role in immunity to disease); and—most ominous of all to modern man—a stomach covered by bleeding ulcers.

Some of the instant, intricate chain of responses in Selye's adapta-

Signals to mobilize the body

Ready to dive, an Olympic contestant responds to the stress of competition by consciously tensing his muscles. Unconsciously, his brain reacts to the same stress by triggering a tiny section, the hypothalamus, to control involuntary muscles and organs through nerve signals and the glandular secretions that are called hormones. The hypothalamus works through two divisions of the autonomic nervous system. Sympathetic nerves, which organize activity, pass from the spinal cord to specific organs through large ganglia, or nerve clusters. These subsidiary switching centers, some scientists speculate, enable sympathetic nerves to mobilize the entire body for quick action. The second division, the parasympathetic nerves, brings the body back to normal; it runs directly from spinal cord to organs.

Directed by the hypothalamus, sympathetic nerves contort facial muscles and widen the eye pupils, nostrils and throat. Within the torso, they adjust the blood supply and relax the stomach, intestines and bladder. Meanwhile, the hypothalamus activates the pituitary gland to send hormones to thyroid and adrenal glands, which release their own secretions. Thyroid hormone steps up energy production, while adrenal hormones increase the supply of fuel by regulating liver, pancreas, spleen and large blood vessels.

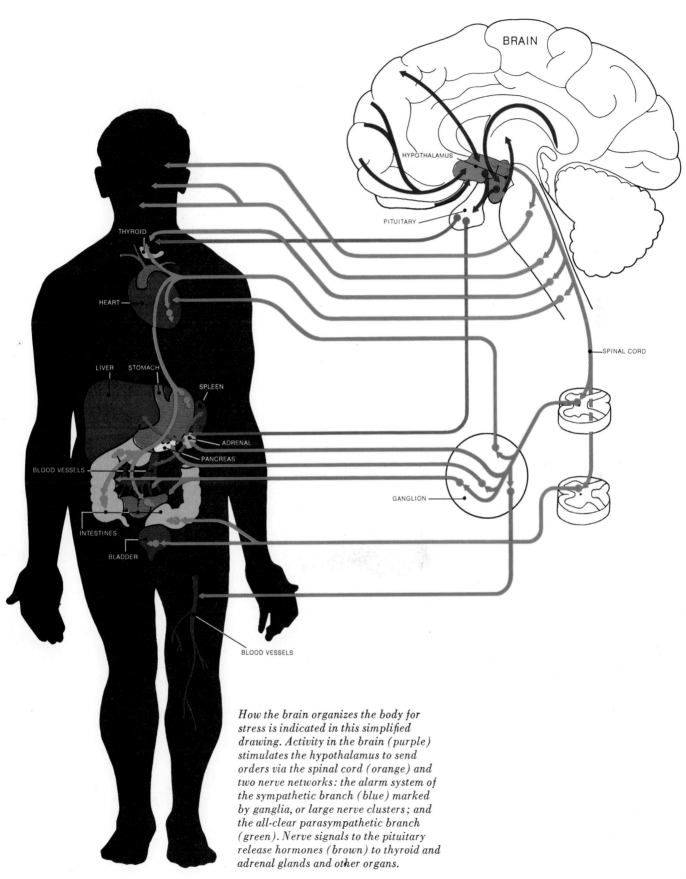

BRAIN

HYPOTHALAMUS

PITUITARY

THYROID

HEART

LIVER STOMACH

SPLEEN

ADRENAL

PANCREAS

BLOOD VESSELS

INTESTINES

BLADDER

BLOOD VESSELS

SPINAL CORD

GANGLION

How the brain organizes the body for stress is indicated in this simplified drawing. Activity in the brain (purple) stimulates the hypothalamus to send orders via the spinal cord (orange) and two nerve networks: the alarm system of the sympathetic branch (blue) marked by ganglia, or large nerve clusters; and the all-clear parasympathetic branch (green). Nerve signals to the pituitary release hormones (brown) to thyroid and adrenal glands and other organs.

tion syndrome, evolved over millions of years, served man's Stone Age ancestors admirably. The alarm reaction of fight or flight made them ready in a flash to combat at peak efficiency or to run away, depending on their evaluation of the odds. Moreover, the physical exertion of a hunt served to burn up accumulated fuel and so release emotional tensions; the hunters could return to camp with pleasantly tired bodies and feelings of satisfaction or triumph. But once men settled down in complex, regulated societies, they found that neither the challenges nor the ways of meeting them were quite so simple. For thousands of years it has not been considered good form to club a competitor over the head or to run away from him in cowardly disgrace. Some parts of the stress response are almost comically inappropriate to modern situations: it does not help a businessman sweating over a budget to have super-acute hearing or quick-clotting blood.

Yet human stress has been complicated not so much by the recent development of modern technological ways of life as by the far earlier advent of human ways of life. Man's highly developed brain, his accumulated knowledge and his ability to communicate and perceive by symbols lead him to find unpleasant or pleasant connotations in an incredible number of situations and events. A human being reacts not only to tangible, physical stresses like heat, cold, immobilization or injury, but also to all manner of symbolic or imagined threats or pleasures. The effect of the stimulus can vary widely, depending on a man's culture, his personal and family background and experiences, and his mood and circumstances at the time. And always, the objective nature of an event or situation is not nearly as important as its meaning to a particular individual at a particular moment.

Even the stress of pain can have meaning that depends more on the significance of the pain than its severity. Civilian surgical patients often complain of severe postoperative discomfort, but combat soldiers with comparably serious wounds may take their pain with a smile. H. K. Beecher, who studied hospitalized soldiers during World War II, reported he was "astonished to find that when the wounded were carried into combat hospitals, only one out of three complained of enough pain to require morphine. Most of the soldiers either denied having pain from their extensive wounds or had so little that they did not want any medication to relieve it. These men," Beecher said, "were not unable to feel pain, for they complained as vigorously as normal men at an inept vein puncture." Why, then, did these soldiers not suffer the pain of their wounds? The answer, Beecher concluded, lay in the meaning of the injury. What a wounded soldier often felt, Beecher decided, "was relief, thankfulness at his escape alive from the battlefield, even euphoria; to the civilian, his major surgery was a depressing, calamitous event."

The human brain has such an influence on the nature of stress partly because it endows men with two broad capacities that are almost, if not entirely, lacking in other animals. One is the ability to control events in the environment. A man, unlike other creatures, does not ordinarily suffer severe stress if he feels cold or hungry; he knows he can put on a jacket to get warm or go to the refrigerator for a snack. He may be severely stressed by loud noise—but less so if he knows he has the power to reduce the noise, whether he actually does reduce it or not.

The second human capacity that affects stress is the ability to look ahead. Like no other creature on earth, man anticipates, always trying to prepare for new situations. Anticipation has a profound influence on stress, and the kind of influence depends not only on the stress but also on the amount and kind of anticipation. A certain amount of anticipation cushions unpleasant reactions and strengthens pleasant ones. But either too little or too much of it makes reactions more intense.

The anticipation of an event can be more stressful than the event itself, as a study of parachute jumpers *(pages 26-27)* made clear: they experienced their greatest stress not while falling through the air but before they left the airplane. Not only the brain but also the body comes to a state of alert in anticipation of such events. Scientists at the U.S. Air Force School of Medicine measured pulse rate and hormone secretion in subjects about to receive a pin prick or the jab of a hypodermic. They found that the mere expectation of pain was enough to generate all the symptoms even if the needle never touched the skin. Nor does an event have to befall an individual directly to make its effect. In an experiment at the University of California, industrial safety films containing simulated shop accidents were shown to a group of subjects. Merely knowing that they were about to witness a worker apparently losing a finger in a machine sent the subjects' heart rates climbing. And though there was some additional rise at the moment the accident flashed on the screen, most of the stress reaction in the subjects' bodies occurred well before the accident was seen.

Much the same anticipatory stress has been observed in students confronting examinations, particularly when the tests are critical ones. A University of Wisconsin researcher found that during the weekend before final examinations psychosomatic symptoms began to show up, with many students reporting stomach-aches, anxiety, asthma, skin rashes or allergies. On the morning of the tests, some experienced acute stomach

Angry antagonists in a Frankfurt, Germany, rooming house engage in a shouting match as each accuses the other of shirking communal cleaning chores. Such confrontations are extremely stressful. They force an individual to choose among three alternatives, all undesirable: he can stand and fight, shrug off the incident, or flee. These elderly disputants chose combat even though their noisy quarrel on the staircase echoed throughout the entire building.

The agonized expression on the face of Frank De Vito betrays his reaction to a stress that most people would welcome. The Sayreville, New Jersey, plumber and his wife have just learned that he won one million dollars in a state lottery.

pains, diarrhea or even trouble in holding down their breakfasts. Yet most of the subjects reported that their symptoms virtually disappeared once they got started on the examination itself. As one student explained, "Taking it is not as bad as anticipating it; you don't have time to worry while you are doing it."

If anticipation can amplify stress, the lack of it does so even more. The unanticipated event—enjoyable or disastrous—has the greatest impact, and sometimes leaves long-lasting aftereffects. A familiar example is the near-miss accident that most people experience more than once in their lives, as likely as not behind the wheel of a car. An automobile races out of a side street, or a child runs into the road from behind a parked car. In a moment, an unconscious stress reaction takes over. Instinctively, the driver jams on the brakes and swerves with apparent coolness and control. Only when the danger is gone—perhaps seconds later, perhaps minutes or even hours—do the signs of a severe stress reaction appear. They may take the form of trembling, faintness, perspiration or even nausea.

The shakiness, the fantasies about what might have happened and the attempts to resolve conflicting emotions can continue to recur in waking hours and in dreams for days following the event. In the instant stress of the emergency the mind and body mobilized unconsciously to meet it; the driver had no time to think. Later, when the full significance of the event sinks in, the adrenalin continues to pump; the stress response does not dissipate rapidly even though there is no further work for it to do.

Most people adjust their behavior to the everyday strains of life, dealing as best they can with mortgages, memos and mothers-in-law, and whether or not they can afford a vacation at the shore—in the psychologist's term, they stay within their adaptive range. Blood pressure may rise when the monthly bank statement arrives mixed up by a computer or the car stalls on a rainy night, but the result is little more than momentary anger. Yet stresses pile up and can push behavior over the adaptive range. Oddly, there is also a bottom limit to this range, and too little stress has profound effects. When the needle on the strain gauge goes either too high or too low, there may be trouble ahead.

At the high end of the scale, when a person encounters an extremely demanding situation, the first reaction is usually anxiety, a varying mixture of alertness, anticipation, curiosity and fear that sets off a search for new information and solutions. The result can be more than the alleviation of anxiety. If one way is blocked, the individual may turn to another, possibly fusing two or more ideas, and the outcome may be very productive. It often seems that worthwhile art, important discovery and inspired performance require the challenging goad of stress.

As anxiety mounts and the needle approaches the danger zone, however, less welcome symptoms can appear. When an individual is faced with a state of overload—with information piling up faster than the mind can process it, and no apparent solutions—his ability to improvise deteriorates, and his behavior regresses to simpler, more primitive responses summoned up from the past. A cautious person, under stress, becomes more cautious; a fleer flees, actually or symbolically. Psychologists classify such reactions as avoidance, denial or "dissonance reduction"—all essentially ostrich-like, often dangerous attempts to pretend that a problem does not exist, or that it will soon go away. However, if a person is a gambler by nature he will gamble; if he is a fighter he will fight. In crisis, each falls back on the solution he knows best.

But it is not necessarily the best solution for anyone. Regardless of personality type, people under high stress show less ability to tolerate ambiguity and to sort out the trivial from the important. Their attack upon a set task becomes uncertain and random; they make more and more mistakes. In an experiment at the University of Maryland, students were asked to identify geometrical forms—stars, circles, triangles —alternately using names and arbitrary code numbers. During the test, however, the scientists deliberately relieved some students of stress and imposed a high stress on others. They told the first group that the tests were interesting but not very important, and that in any case the students were doing quite well. The other subjects were told that their performance so far was poor, and that they had better realize that these tests were considered indicators of success in the university and might be used as a screening device. From that point on, the first, unstressed group worked better and faster. The second began to "block," hesitating between alternatives; total time for the tests rose accordingly, and the error rate soared.

Far more serious than errors on a test are other behavior changes that, some experts believe, follow prolonged overloads of stress. Adaptive energy, in Hans Selye's terms, may be exhausted. And like Selye's fatally overstressed rats, men have been killed, according to some authorities, by direct stress. The evidence for such extreme impact of overloads is still controversial *(Chapter 4)*, but there is little doubt that too much stress at once, or even a little stress for too long, can impair physical and emotional well-being.

If people cannot long tolerate stress overload, neither can they tolerate severe underload. Too little of the external stimuli considered stressful may presage symptoms that, paradoxically, are similar to those of stress. It seems that the absence of stress is itself a kind of stress. For example, rats, monkeys and children raised without handling and normal discipline from their mothers grow stunted and vulnerable. The young almost always are fearful, mentally and emotionally retarded and unable to handle even the simplest challenge; they have not had enough stimulation, enough exercise of body and brain, to learn to behave normally.

Both planned experiment and practical experience have repeatedly demonstrated the profound emotional changes brought about by the deliberate isolation of men from the stresses imposed by society. People who must spend long periods alone develop bizarre symptoms. "Cabin fever" is a recognized phenomenon among solitary trappers of the North. Many explorers, shipwrecked sailors and men who attempt solo sea voyages have reported episodes of acute depression, panic and hallucinations. Pilots flying alone at high altitudes occasionally experience a "breakaway effect," a weird feeling of losing all contact with the earth and even with their own bodies. Truck drivers droning along for hours on monotonous highways have sworn they have seen jack rabbits as big as elephants bounding alongside their trucks.

Even the most comfortable isolation from normal stimuli is distasteful, and if the isolation is nearly complete, it can be disastrous. This odd fact seems to contradict common sense, since most people long for an extended period of peace and quiet. But there is no doubt that depriving humans of sensations from outside their bodies has profound effects on behavior. The phenomenon was first demonstrated in the early 1950s at McGill University in Montreal by Donald O. Hebb, who immobilized blindfolded students in comfortable beds. His findings that sensory deprivation was unbearable astonished scientists. "Unlike so many pallid experimental situations," commented psychologist Peter Suedfeld, this one made "a difference you could almost taste."

Since Hebb's pioneering tests, many other experimenters have duplicated and extended his work. They have put subjects into soundproof cubicles and iron-lung respirators; shut off their sight with darkness, goggles, eye patches and even halved table-tennis balls taped over their eyes; blocked hearing with insulated chambers, earplugs, earphones and background hums; and muffled their sense of touch with gloves and cuffs. Invariably the subjects demanded to be released from isolation within a few days at most. Most of them reported hallucinations, and

A frightened boy breaks down before a hand has been laid on him while waiting to be inoculated against measles in a Fairfax, Virginia, clinic. For him and for others who must face an unpleasant or unfamiliar experience, anticipation can be the severest form of stress.

Parachuting to earth

Jumping

About to jump

Ready to jump

Boarding plane

At airport

Morning of jump

This graph traces changes in the anxiety felt by two groups of parachute jumpers in the stages shown on these pages. In the graph, zero represents no anxiety, nine the highest level.

The morning of the jump, *raking leaves before deciding to go, the experienced jumper is twice as anxious as an inexperienced one (graph, left).*

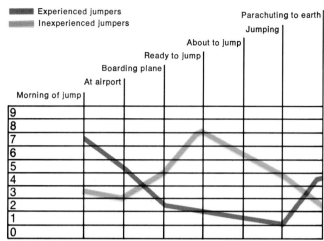

At the airport, *the experienced jumper still displays more anxiety than the novice, but his fears are lessening. The beginner's fears, however, are about to increase.*

The old pro's well-founded fear

Anxiety can be both beneficial and treacherous. Moderate amounts of fear are a protection, but fear unchecked can paralyze. To learn about anxiety— and find ways to control it—psychologist Seymour Epstein tested two groups of parachutists, one experienced, the other inexperienced. Each jumper was asked how fear-ridden he had been at certain times.

The results, as shown here along with stills from a movie by Epstein, were surprising. The veterans suffered their highest levels of anxiety hours before the jump, while the beginners' fear became significant only at the airport. After the jump, however, the veterans again worried more.

Boarding the airplane, *both groups change dramatically. While the veteran has inhibited his fears, the novice is gradually becoming more and more apprehensive.*

Ready to jump, *the novice has reached his highest state of anxiety. The experienced parachutist continues to be relaxed, his mind almost rid of worry.*

About to jump, *outside the plane but with one foot on a step, the beginner begins to lose some of his anxieties. The crucial decision is already behind him.*

Jumping, *the veteran sails euphorically, anxiety at its lowest level. The beginner is four times more anxious—even though his fears continue to dwindle.*

Parachuting to earth, *the beginning jumper's worries are over, but the veteran parachuter suffers a final twinge of fear as his control over his anxieties lessens.*

their abilities to reason and to judge time and distance were impaired, in some cases for days after the experiment ended.

One of the most convincing—and unusual—of these experiments in "sensory deprivation" was reported by Jay T. Shurley, Professor of Psychiatry at the University of Oklahoma. He suspended men and women of various ages and backgrounds under water in a womblike tank. They could see nothing, hear nothing and feel nothing. They sensed neither cold nor heat, since the water was just about at body temperature, and very gently flowing. They could not even detect the pull of gravity—that is, the weight of their own bodies—for carefully positioned ballast kept them neutrally buoyant, suspended within the water. Face masks provided low-pressure, low-humidity air, odor-free, at 70° F. None of the subjects could stand it for more than six hours.

Shurley reported as typical the reactions of a journalist, who volunteered for the test to get material for a story. In the tank his thoughts rambled while he whistled, sang and talked almost continuously—in four and a half hours he was never quiet longer than six minutes. He heard men talking and dogs barking, sensed the presence of a nonexistent companion, vacillated between gaiety and depression, and saw a light that "looked like sun through a peephole." After he left the tank, he acted exhilarated and pleased by the experience—until the end of his interview with the scientist. The journalist said then: "I honestly believe, if you put a person in there, just kept him and fed him by vein, he'd just flat die." And he never did the story.

Through such sensory-deprivation experiments it has become apparent that the nervous system needs a constant level of stimulation to function. Deprived of a normal range of incoming information, the system compensates by creating its own stimuli. It seizes upon any signals it can find, even those from brain and body. If the faint signals are somewhat pleasant, they can be magnified into irrational feelings of pure joy; if they are disturbing, they can turn into vivid experiences of horror and pain.

Such problems do not arise in the course of normal daily living. The mind constantly regulates and edits the amount of stimulation it receives in order to maintain a steady, satisfying level of stress. Underloads are turned up, overloads turned down or dissipated. If a stress becomes too great it can often be pushed aside or relieved by any means from a long walk to mystic introspection *(Chapter 5)*—or an emotional outburst. Physiologist Stewart Wolf of the University of Texas reported the case of a patient whose blood pressure had been consistently high for years. It could be made to go even higher by discussing the patient's stressful relationship with an acquaintance. The only time a normal pressure was recorded in the patient occurred immediately after he beat up his tormentor.

When stress levels fall too low for normal stimulation, people seek excitement in work and play. Some take up chess or bridge, others read exciting stories or go to disaster movies, still others drive fast cars. There are those who seem to thrive on constant stress. Hollywood and the business novel have perpetuated one classic stereotype of stress: the harried, hard-driving executive who one day doubles up with ulcers. The image fascinates some readers and movie-goers, but it is by no means the whole picture. "I don't get ulcers," a famous real-estate tycoon used to tell visitors to his penthouse office, as he looked down upon the Manhattan skyline with a beatific smile; "I *give* them." There is persuasive evidence, in fact, that many of those who reach the top do so largely because they have learned how to manage stress and use it to advantage—in themselves and others—and that they have fewer hangups, breakdowns or heart attacks than middle managers and workers still farther down the corporate ladder.

Such successful executives are among many active stress-seekers —politicians, athletes, entertainers and ordinary folk who find personal fulfillment in pressure, competition, danger and the roar of the crowd. Staid bankers climb mountains; librarians fly airplanes or canoe through rapids on their days off. One such stress-seeker is Sol Roy Rosenthal, Medical Director of Chicago's Research Foundation, a dedicated horseman who at the age of 72 still goes fox hunting over fields and fences three times a week. Rosenthal describes his sport, and such equally demanding sports as sky-diving, as "high-risk exercise," pointing out that they produce a euphoria that no others can.

For the stress-seeker, it is as though the hormones of his stress response—his own hormones—become an addictive drug. The addiction seems to be strongest in skilled athletes, whose triumphs and defeats are shared vicariously by spectators balancing their own diets of stress. In a study of such "stimulus addicts," psychologist Bruce Ogilvie of California's San Jose State University gave personality tests to some 300 athletes, including professional football players, stunt pilots, racing-car drivers, parachutists, fencers, basketball players and Olympic swimmers. He found that as a group they ranked unusually high in intelligence, ambition, emotional stability and leadership. "For such people," Ogilvie concluded, "to live a life uncontested is tantamount to have only half-lived."

People who seek stress

After England's Roger Bannister became the first man to run a mile in four minutes, he described the feelings he had experienced as "joy in struggle, freedom in toil, satisfaction at the mental and physical cost." It was the classic account of the emotions of the "stress-seeker," a term coined by psychologist-sociologist Samuel Z. Klausner to denote people who deliberately immerse themselves in stress.

To such persons, Klausner explains, the deliberate courting of stress brings the feeling of being intensely alive. Some, like Bannister, achieve this state by pitting themselves against difficult or even threatening situations. Others find the same stimulation by becoming part of a celebrating crowd, such as the youthful audiences that throng to attend rock concerts. Or the sensation may be sought in esthetic or intellectual effort.

Whatever the nature of the stress sought, those who seek it share certain characteristics, Klausner found. Their behavior is carefully planned; the novelist Ernest Hemingway not only analyzed stress-seeking in print *(page 32)*, but was an avid practitioner himself —he went to war three times, hunted big game and climbed into the ring with prize fighters. But none of these situations was entered blindly. When, at the age of 49, Hemingway decided to try his hand at lion-taming, he did so only after he had made friends with a trainer, who supervised every encounter with the big cats.

Stress-seekers repeatedly return to the stressful situation: in 1954, one year after Sir Edmund Hillary became the first man to climb Mount Everest, he went back to tackle more peaks.

Striving toward the finish, hurdlers strain to snap through their jumps without losing speed at an Olympics tryout in California. Their effort is emphasized in this picture by the elongated, streaking effect created by the photographer, who used a camera containing moving film to stretch out the runners' images.

In an arduous but exhilarating ascent, a California rock climber nears an overhang.

A deliberate quest for physical danger

"First a crowd came down the street, running packed close together," wrote Ernest Hemingway of the running of the bulls in Pamplona, Spain *(right)*, "behind them came more men running faster, and then some stragglers who were really running." No one doubts what makes these young men race a herd of fighting bulls to the ring during the annual fiesta. They purposely expose themselves to physical danger to prove their own worth to themselves.

The need to win over the stress of fear is the driving force in many sports from auto-racing to mountain-climbing *(above)*. "Why climb a mountain?" is the famous question once put to expert George Leigh Mallory; his answer: "Because it's there."

Only paces ahead of a herd of galloping bulls, a man at Pamplona proves his mettle by outracing the animals to the town bull ring.

The tensions of creativity

At a 1966 conference on stress-seeking, psychologist E. Paul Torrance suggested that stress is a major factor behind the achievements of many great artists. Instead of just adapting or adjusting to their environment, they deliberately expose themselves to stressful conditions, said Torrance.

Torrance might have been talking specifically about pianist Vladimir Horowitz *(right)*, whose passion for self-improvement is renowned; he never plays the same piece the same way twice but pushes himself to find new interpretations of distinguished originality. While critics praise his playing, Horowitz himself remains dissatisfied. "The struggle for perfection is never-ending" he says.

His face furrowed by intense effort, Vladimir Horowitz ponders his playing of a Chopin rondo during a rehearsal for a 1974 recital.

Two men indulge in a time-honored form of interpersonal stress-seeking as they play a Chinese version of chess in Shanghai's Palace.

A Wisconsin student goads a policeman during a tense moment at a 1967 antiwar protest.

Person-to-person encounters

Disguised by the controlled behavior of the chess players at left is the severe stress of interpersonal conflict, for such a coldly intellectual match is really a fierce form of competition. World chess champion Anatoly Karpov spoke plainly about his own motivation: "It is the opposition of two wills," adding, "It is this struggle that makes the game so attractive."

Desire for the same struggle of wills has led the youth above to provoke a police officer. Though he is inviting injury or arrest, such an invitation is generally so presented that it will be almost but not quite accepted. According to Klausner, usually the stress-seeker chooses an adversary he can go up against without being destroyed.

An individual confronting a crowd

Always exhausting, often dangerous, the press of the crowd is vital sustenance to many of the most successful political leaders. During Robert Kennedy's 1968 campaign for the Presidency *(right)*, crowds in Indiana became so demonstrative that they forced him up against a car, breaking a front tooth. President Lyndon Johnson, an incorrigible hand-shaker, often emerged from enthusiastic mobs of well-wishers with bleeding fingers.

But the emotional lift of such moments is worth the effort: a reporter traveling with the President noted that he seemed to "drink in huge draughts of adoration from the crowds. Each foray into their midst seemed like a narcotic that required constant renewal."

Buoyed up by the crowd, Robert Kennedy begins the physically agonizing ritual of shaking thousands of hands at a Philadelphia rally.

Pressures of Daily Life

2

"The difficulties of adjustment to the stress and strain of contemporary living," said psychiatrist Karl Menninger, "have been bemoaned and deplored by every generation since long before the Christian era." The prize for lamentation, however, must surely go to the present articulate Age of Anxiety. Its problems are proclaimed daily, in living color and in a best-selling literature of turmoil, alienation and despair. Sometimes the stresses of modern life seem too much to bear. In secret moments many people yearn to chuck the agonies of rush-hour commuting *(left)* no less than the dread of nuclear war and move to the mountains, or a farm community or the rose-covered cottage of dreams.

Are the stresses and strains of modern society really that much worse than they were in the good old days—or do they just seem that way? The evidence is strangely conflicting. Some modern stresses seem to be enjoyable ones. Others affect people one way in one culture, another way in other cultures.

Looking back longingly in history's rearview mirror, it is easy to forget that, by and large, the old days were not all that good. Despite some musical comedies to the contrary, life on a pioneer farm in Oklahoma or Saskatchewan was no bed of roses. It consisted of six or seven days a week of pure physical drudgery, starting before sunup and ending with a frugal meal by candlelight, exhaustion, and bed. The round of daily living was lonely, sometimes dangerous and often sorrowful, for neighbors lived far away and medical help was remote and rudimentary. Infant mortality was high, children died one after another from diphtheria and other diseases, and economic disaster was often imminent. There were few luxuries for anyone and even the necessities of life were precarious and uncertain: on a farm raising marginal crops, hailstorms, spring floods or summer drought could wipe out a year's living. Still, to offset these dangers and hardships, a farmer and his family had certain fundamental positive values—most notably, perhaps, a sense of identity with the earth and with one another, and a sense of control over their destiny, which depended mainly on the work of their own hands.

In little more than a century this more or less typical picture of a rural, agrarian society has undergone drastic, almost unbelievable, change. A continuous urbanization, only now leveling off (or perhaps reversing), has transformed the so-called developed nations; about three quarters of their people now live in cities or suburbs, not on farms. The developing nations are rapidly catching up; in the Western Hemisphere alone, according to United Nations projections, such traditionally agrarian countries as Brazil and Mexico will approach the 75-per-cent-urban figure by 1990, and Argentina will surpass it. The shift from the old rural to the modern urban life has made existence easier in some respects, harder in others. In place of plowshares and candlelight there are automobiles, neon signs, television and multinational corporations —and along with these mixed blessings there is also a whole new set of stresses. The old ones were essentially harsh, simple and largely predictable; most of them were rooted in physical threats or deprivations. The new stresses comprise a whole catalogue of psychological irritants, many of them by-products of comfortable standards of living, and either unpredictable or beyond any immediate, individual control. Today, stress is not so much direct and fateful as it is constant, nagging and cumulative. In an alarming number of people, it exacts a heavy price.

Many of the stresses of modern life are so familiar they have come to be accepted because there seems no alternative. The car refuses to start on a cold winter morning, or the refrigerator dies on a broiling summer day. The unlucky owner, lacking knowledge of their complex mechanisms, mutters a curse at the manufacturer and, in a foul temper, goes looking for a repair man. (When his bill comes in, it often brings an extra dividend of stress.) Getting to work, a modern chore not on the farmer's list, is time-consuming at best; at worst it can turn into an unending nightmare: traffic piles up for miles on the road and everyone sits in private, knotted tension; the subway suddenly stalls in a pitch-black tunnel and the passengers wait, perspiring in the fetid air; an outbound commuter train inexplicably breaks down far from home with wives waiting and numberless dinners burning on the stove.

In the city proper there is a paradox. Here is the fulfillment of man's needs and hopes, the wellspring of riches, pleasures, ideas, culture and companionship. Some of these prizes are inherently stressful—the stimulation they provide attracts many people to the city. In other cases pursuit of the prizes exacts a price in stress. For city annoyances are constant, and seldom controllable: crowds to maneuver through, lines to stand in, seats to compete for, faceless bureaucracies to deal with, strikes, demonstrations, crime. Almost everywhere there is noise—the neighbor's radio blaring, the crash of garbage cans at 4 a.m., sirens, jackhammers, horns. And there is ugliness. Compared to the spare simplicity of forest, farm and village, the modern urban landscape is rarely a sight for the sore, smog-burned eyes that gaze upon it; increasingly, all over the world, this landscape seems to consist of the same hopeless jumble of billboards, junk yards, decrepit old buildings and tinny new ones, all set off in a transient, man-made wasteland of wind-blown garbage and vacant lots.

The first to deplore the deteriorating quality of the modern city, and the toll it takes on its inhabitants, were the British, who first felt the impact during the Industrial Revolution. After visiting such burgeoning centers of the textile industry as Manchester, a social historian, William Cooke Taylor, portentously observed that "as a stranger passes through the masses of human beings which have been accumulated around the mills, he cannot contemplate these crowded hives without feelings of anxiety and apprehension amounting almost to dismay. The population is hourly increasing in breadth and strength." The political reformer William Cobbett, writing in the 1820s, suggested that the size and density of the new cities created a breeding ground of corruption. "Jails, barracks, factories," Cobbett argued, "do not corrupt by their walls, but by their condensed numbers. Populous cities corrupt for the same cause."

As the Industrial Revolution spread around the globe, so did complaints about urban life. In America in 1881 a physician, George Beard, discovered a disease he called American nervousness. Its "chief and primary cause," he wrote, "is *modern civilization*, which is distinguished from the ancient by these five characteristics: steam power, the periodical press, the telegraph, the sciences, and the mental activity of women." Of all these, he singled out steam power as the archvillain. Introduced into factories, it had broken down the work of artisans into repetitive and monotonous tasks and had at the same time speeded up manufacturing, pushing men beyond their natural limits.

Clocks and watches, Beard observed, used to tell time in an approximate fashion for those who could afford them; now, accurate and ubiquitous, they drove men just as surely as the steam that turned machines, placing people "under constant strain, mostly unconscious, oftentimes in sleeping as well as waking hours, to get somewhere or to do something at some definite moment." Public conveyances like railroad trains and trolley cars combined with the machines of mills and fac-

Joyously seeking the stress of the city—noise, crowding and tense exhilaration—fans at an open-air rock concert in San Francisco raise arms to salute the performing group, The Grateful Dead.

tories to fill the cities with harsh and jarring sounds that Beard found as debilitating as the most vigorous physical exertions. The telegraph speeded up business transactions and intensified competition, driving some executives beyond their natural limits too. These factors, Beard felt, were exacerbated by the "periodical press." The resulting atmosphere, he found, was one of such rapid change and constant argument that everyone seemed to teeter on the verge of nervous exhaustion.

In the years since these early alarms, experts have not stopped wringing their hands, viewing with alarm and attempting to dissect the multiplying sources of stress in modern life. In 1914 Walter Lippmann, the journalist-philosopher, suggested a cogent explanation in his book *Drift and Mastery:* "We are not used to a complicated civilization. We have changed our environment more quickly than we know how to change ourselves." Half a century later microbiologist-philosopher René Dubos looked at the other side of the coin: "Life in the modern city has become a symbol of the fact that man can become adapted to starless skies, treeless avenues, shapeless buildings, tasteless bread, joyless celebrations, spiritless pleasures. The frightful threat posed by adaptability is that it implies so often a passive acceptance of conditions which really are not desirable for mankind." Others elaborate this theme, but most say the same thing. Behind the wheel of every automobile lurks a Stone Age man. Sometimes he laughs, sometimes he cries, sometimes he snarls at his fellows, but a lot of the time he just sits there, inexplicably marooned in the 20th Century, feeling nervous, tense and irritable. The place he feels this stress most is the crowded, noisy, concrete jungle of the modern city.

Of all the city's characteristics, the most obvious, the most important, and the most potentially stressful is probably crowding. This fact is not surprising; by definition, a city is a place where people congregate to do business with one another, face to face. The degree to which a great city extends face-to-face contacts is often unappreciated, however. A study of the New York area by the Regional Plan Association demonstrated how a centralized city increased the opportunities for personal business contacts. The survey compared a suburban area, Nassau County, with a satellite city, Newark, and the central core of midtown Manhattan. It found, "an office worker in central Nassau County must go to meetings by car. Within 10 minutes from his desk, he can meet with any of 11,000 other employed persons with whom he may have business. This is a measure of the outside services and other links conveniently available. With scattered offices served only by automobile, that number is close to the maximum possible. The Newark office worker usually goes to meetings on foot and can reach more than twice as many employed persons within 10 minutes of his desk. In Midtown Manhattan—even more compact—an office worker can reach 220,000 other employed persons in 10 minutes by subway, bus, taxi and foot."

Without a high population density, the city could not perform its function as a city. But the sinister side of crowding—and its by-products, noise, traffic and pollution—has long been recognized and deplored. In the First Century A.D., when Rome had a population density twice that of Paris today, Julius Caesar concentrated on the traffic problem: he tried to reduce crowding in the city by setting up one-way streets, building parking lots for chariots and forbidding freight wagons to load or unload during the day. In the 19th Century, appalled by the urban squalor of the Industrial Revolution, the poet Percy Shelley suggested that "Hell is a city much like London, a populous and smoky city."

The critics had good cause for despair. Crowding, to begin with, was an indisputable factor in the spread of tuberculosis and other infectious diseases in 19th Century cities. Not only was the tubercle bacillus quickly transmitted from one victim to another under crowded, unsanitary conditions, but also the strains upon the new urban migrants—the disorienting change from rural to urban life, the exhausting hours in mills and mines, the pervasiveness of poverty, inadequate diet and poor housing—lowered their resistance to disease. Indeed, drastic change in times of crisis has always been associated with a marked rise in death from tuberculosis: the disease spread throughout Europe during World War I, even in nations far removed from the combat zones; in earlier years it peaked among immigrants to the United States (the death rate among the Irish in New York City in the mid-19th Century was double that in Dublin), and it killed American Indians when they were jammed into reservations after living on the open plains. With improved sanitation and modern drugs the mortality rate from tuberculosis has dropped dramatically in Western nations, but the same cycle is beginning again in developing nations encountering the stresses of industrialization and urbanization: despite the best efforts of local health programs and the World Health Organization, tuberculosis kills more than three million people a year in Africa, Asia and South America.

Studies of animals living in densely populated pens indicate that not only tuberculosis but also many other diseases of body and mind are brought on by crowding. Biologists have long observed that as deer, muskrats, lemmings and other mammals increase in population beyond the carrying capacity of a given territory, stress eventually triggers reactions in body chemistry that lead to a decrease in fertility, an increase

The ill effects of stress brought on by overcrowding have been repeatedly demonstrated in experiments on animals like these huddled mice. Rejected by mothers that were disturbed by life in a densely populated pen, the mice never learned mature behavior. They did not participate in the activities of their more aggressive fellows below.

in the death rate and a resulting decline in population. Observations on a small island off the Maryland coast revealed that the rapid expansion of a herd of deer to 300 members was quickly followed by a contraction to 100 survivors; the dead animals were found to have enlarged adrenal glands and signs of chronic kidney disease—both related to stress. A comparable study of animals in crowded cages at the Philadelphia Zoo indicated that they usually died of perforated ulcers and chronic heart disease, ailments that also affect humans under stress.

The physical and mental effects of crowding have been studied extensively in animals under controlled laboratory conditions. Perhaps the best known of these experiments were conducted over a period of years by John Calhoun at the Laboratory of Psychology of the United States National Institute of Mental Health. In one experiment Calhoun placed five pregnant Norway rats in a large, quarter-acre pen equipped with built-in "apartments" for nesting and all the food and water that an expanding population could possibly need. These resources, used efficiently, should have been sufficient to support 5,000 rats. But even after 27 months the population never increased beyond 150. What had gone wrong? Calhoun discovered that a few dominant males had staked out their own spacious territories and defended them and their mates from all comers. The rest of the rats lived, slept and ate in a confused mass. Some of the crowded males formed gangs to attack females; other males confused their own sex, mounting males as well as females; still others became totally passive and withdrawn; a few turned vicious and even cannibalistic. Fighting became so disruptive that some females had miscarriages, some reabsorbed full-grown fetuses before they could be born, and those that did bear young became too distracted to tend them; many infants died of neglect.

Calhoun termed this condition of bedlam and mayhem the result of a "behavioral sink," which he defined as "any behavioral process that collects animals together in unusually great numbers." In such a sink, he found that for rats, at least, it was always "women and children first" —to die. The mortality rate of females was three and a half times that of the males; of 558 young rats born in one such experimental sink, only one quarter survived to be weaned. Many females died during pregnancy and birth, and their kidneys, livers and adrenal glands proved to be enlarged by disease.

From studies like Calhoun's, it is clear that animals, at least, suffer when crowded. But what about man? Researchers have had far less success applying such cause-and-effect relationships to humans, the most adaptable of all creatures. Statistics from many cities do show that dis-

proportionately high rates of crime, drug abuse and mental illness occur when human beings are packed together. But there is much dispute about the influence crowding, as such, has on these problems.

In the early 1970s, for example, sociologists and psychiatrists at London's Bedford College interviewed a random sample of 220 women in Camberwell, a working-class district in South London with a population density roughly twice that of the Greater London Area as a whole. None of the women had ever received psychiatric care—but the interviewers found that over a third of their sample either needed such care or were borderline cases with definite symptoms of psychological disorder. During the 1960s the so-called Midtown Manhattan Study, conducted in New York by psychologists and sociologists at the Cornell Medical School, had come up with even more startling statistics. The Cornell scientists surveyed about 2,000 residents of the city between Park Avenue and the East River from 59th to 96th Street—an ethnically and economically diverse area in which the average population density ran to 600 people per acre, four times that of the city's central core as a whole and 130 times that of New York's most lightly settled section. Four out of every five people surveyed had symptoms of psychiatric disorder; roughly one out of four had neuroses severe enough to disrupt their daily lives. And compared with the city-wide averages, midtown had twice as much suicide, accidental death, tuberculosis and juvenile delinquency, and three times as much alcoholism.

But neither the Camberwell nor the Midtown Manhattan survey was able to establish whether crowding was responsible for the conditions uncovered. Similarly, no scientific study has ever successfully indicated what proportion of such ills are traceable to overcrowding and what proportion to other factors—unemployment, poverty, unstable family life or the general hopelessness of getting out of a slum. Does crowding create pathology, or does it simply make pathology easier to see, to study, to report and tabulate? Does the city create afflicted, antisocial people, or does it attract and provide a haven for them?

For the moment, such questions are unanswerable. But if any one fact about crowding is certain, it is that its effects on humans depend on many things besides the mere density of people per acre. How people perceive crowding varies from person to person, man to woman, nation to nation and situation to situation.

In many circumstances crowding is an asset, even a prerequisite to success, because it heightens the stimulation and pleasure of an event. Part of the color and appeal of the shopping, restaurant and theater districts of a city is their very crowdedness, and the excitement that comes from rubbing elbows with a wide variety of people. A theatergoer on opening night would experience acute discomfort, perhaps outright panic, if he found himself the only customer. In many circles a cocktail party is a failure if the guests do not form a noisy, pulsating throng, packed so tightly they can barely squeeze past one another. The person who expects to have a good time in crowded conditions probably will. If he finds the play or the party boring or even distressing, it will not last forever—and he can always leave. Control over the duration of stress greatly influences its effect. Most people can tolerate extreme crowding of an unpleasant nature if its duration is predictable and reasonably short. The maximum legal capacity of a New York City subway car, which often seems more exceeded than observed, provides each passenger with 20.8 cubic feet—less than the Black Hole of Calcutta, which allowed about 22. And though the Black Hole and the subway have been likened to each other, especially by ruffled out-of-towners, subway riders submit to the ordeal twice daily and manage to stay alive.

The extent to which the stresses of urban life depend on the individual's sense of control, or lack of it, becomes clear in studies of commuting, certainly one of the more stressful burdens of urban life. In an experiment designed to establish relationships between stress and heart disease, physicians attached pulse counters to the wrists of a group of hard-working executives and asked them to note down readings and activities periodically. One of the subjects, a newspaper editor who commuted from the suburbs daily by automobile to San Francisco, was astonished to discover the impact of the trip. He had assumed, sensibly enough, that his pulse would be fastest at work, when the presses broke down in the middle of a run, when a front page had to be made over to accommodate a news event or, perhaps, during a particularly frustrating budget session with the owners of the paper. Not so. His most stressful activity, as measured by peaks on the pulse counter, was driving to and from work—dodging cars, competing for position, getting caught helplessly in traffic—situations over which he had almost no control.

Even during a trip to work on a comfortable commuter train, the stresses turn out to depend on the passengers' control over their ride. In

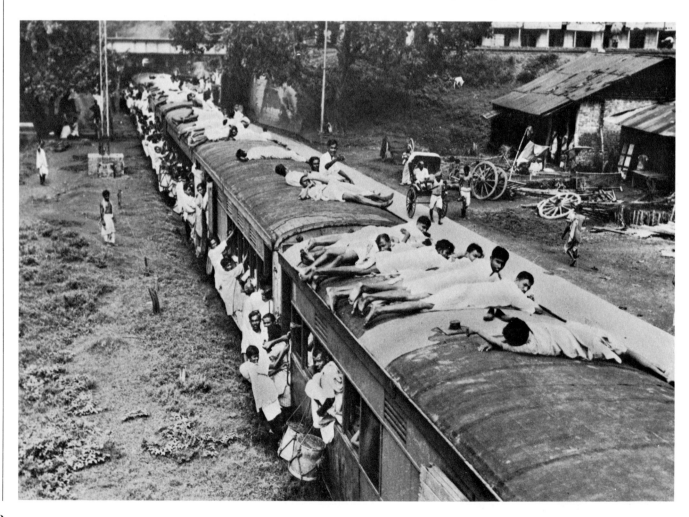

a study of Sweden's Nynäshamm-Stockholm line, psychologists divided the passengers into two groups: those who boarded the train at the beginning of the ride, in Nynäshamm, and those who got on at a station midway between Nynäshamm and Stockholm. On four successive mornings, both groups reported about their reactions to traveling on the train. These reports indicated their subjective feelings about the journey—but as in San Francisco, the researchers took a further step. As material for an objective check on stress, they collected urine samples from the passengers before and after the trip; the levels of a stress-related body compound, the adrenal hormone epinephrine, like the pulse rates in San Francisco, would show the subjects' real stress peaks.

In the interviews, all the riders agreed that as the train trip grew longer and more time-consuming, it also became more crowded and aggravating. But analyses of the hormone levels told a different story. The subjects who got on at the start of the line for the 79-minute ride to downtown Stockholm experienced significantly less stress than the midstation passengers, who had only a 43-minute trip. The key to this contrast between subjective feelings and objective facts, the researchers found, was largely a question of control and freedom of choice. Commuters boarding the train at the first stop, when the cars were empty, had the greatest choice of seats. They could arrange their coats, briefcases and parcels in the way that pleased them, and they could choose particular acquaintances to sit with or to avoid, depending on how they felt that day. The people who got on at the midway station, by contrast, scrambled for the seats that were left, which might mean squeezing in next to a fat man, maneuvering around a loudly snoring sleeper or finding the overhead luggage racks full.

The stress of crowding, then, is not so much a matter of density as of a loss of control. Psychologist Jonathan Freedman of New York's Columbia University finds that people do not even become aware of density or a feeling of being crowded until the situation begins to restrict their options, to interfere with their objectives at a given moment. A driver stuck in traffic, a train rider trying to find a seat, a shopper pushing his way to the sales counter—in each case, an inadequate amount of available space disrupts what a person intends to do or causes more forced social interaction than a person cares for, and crowding becomes stressful. A man might seek the company of thousands to jostle with on New Year's Eve; the same man might well lose his temper at the thought of losing his privacy by sharing his office with a single fellow employee.

While control over crowding always seems the major factor in determining the degree of stress, certain categories of people differ

On a train so jammed they must cling to the roof and sides, Calcutta-bound workers endure a major stress of city life —crowded, hazardous commuting—as they make their way to their jobs. Commuting strains, one study found, are worse than those of a tension-filled job. The Calcutta lines carry 800,000 riders each day; 19 of them died in 1974.

A society in thrall to its services

For 13 weeks in the spring of 1975, residents of Glasgow picked their way along sidewalks strewn with mounds of garbage. About 75,000 tons of debris littered the streets, and troops of the Royal Highland Fusiliers had to be called in to haul away the glut.

Such a garbage strike cannot frustrate an old-fashioned farmer because he has no garbage man. But in the city, municipal services are a vital part of daily life and their absence imposes exceptional stress on the urbanite because he is powerless to replace them. The strike of a few elevator repairmen, for example, can maroon helpless residents in upper-floor apartments.

This loss of control can foster a vig-

orous reaction that may be futile. Yet it is nonetheless satisfying because it expresses the primordial response to threatening stress: fight back. When a transportation strike in 1974 stranded thousands of London commuters, they lost their stiff upper lips and cornered one engineer in his cab, under siege, until he was rescued by police.

An opposite but equally ancient response to stress was displayed by the citizens of Buenos Aires when a general strike immobilized that city of eight million. The strike lost much of its effectiveness when the strikers found that the public welcomed the chance to take a short vacation; great crowds of them headed for the beach.

Venetians are left marooned on their doorsteps as 400 irate gondoliers jam the Grand Canal to protest speeding motorboats that joggle gondolas in backwash. The demonstrators halted all canal traffic until the city rushed through a speed limit on the motorboats.

A Londoner needs no coaching to hold his nose for the photographer as he passes refuse uncollected during a six-week strike. Garbage strikes are a recurrent plague in many cities—including Venice, where sanitation scows, like the gondolas opposite, blockaded the Grand Canal.

In Paris, where food is taken seriously and shoppers grab vegetables out of one another's hands during grocers' strikes, disconsolate customers wander past supermarket shelves that were newly emptied by hoarding housewives during a general work stoppage in 1968.

markedly in their reactions to it. Men are affected differently from women, Freedman found. When subjects were left together in rooms of adequate size for periods up to four hours and asked to work on problems and take part in discussions, their behavior and reasoning processes were not generally impaired by the proximity of others. But when smaller rooms were used and crowding increased, subjects in all-male groups seemed to like each other less and became more competitive and aggressive; in a test that simulated a jury trial, the men handed out increasingly severe verdicts when they were confined in smaller rooms. Women in all-female groups, on the other hand, actually seemed to prefer the smaller spaces; they responded to one another and to the plight of the defendant more positively and warmly when they were placed closer together.

The thesis that men prefer more space and women less is supported by psychologist Michael Ross of Canada's University of Waterloo, who

had groups of men and women carry on discussions and fill out questionnaires in both large and small rooms. Men, it turned out, rated themselves and others more highly on such traits as likeability and imagination in the large room, and looked directly into people's faces more often; in the smaller room, apparently finding things a bit too close for comfort, they attempted to increase the psychological distance between themselves and others by averting their eyes. Women, in contrast, rated themselves more highly in the small room and maintained more eye contact with others than in the larger room.

Jonathan Freedman advances no fewer than four alternative hypotheses to account for these differences between men and women. First, he suggests that males of every species are naturally more territorial than females. Second, because males are generally larger and more physically active than females, they need more space around them. Third, close physical contact is accepted as a condition of friendship and intimacy among women, but tends to create threatening or homosexual overtones among men. And fourth—the hypothesis Freedman favors —men and women respond differently not to crowding as such but to members of their own sex; crowding merely heightens their response.

The differences in male and female reactions to crowding are subtle. Much more obvious are the variations introduced by culture. Human concentrations that are stressful in one nation are in another endured with no apparent special effect. Contacts unacceptable in one are desired in another.

The anthropologist Edward T. Hall observed that Frenchmen, Italians, Greeks, Arabs and Japanese have a much higher tolerance for public crowding than do Englishmen, Germans, Scandinavians and many Americans. In effect, Hall said, an individual exists within an invisible bubble of "personal space," which varies in size depending on the person, his culture and the situation. When this bubble is violated the individual experiences varying amounts of stress. An Englishman talking to a Frenchman, whatever their relationship, may feel that the latter is moving in too close, breathing in his face and about to spit at any moment, while the Frenchman may wonder why the cold Englishman keeps moving back where he cannot be reached with the full force of the argument. Psychiatrists have found that the bubble can grow considerably in size as a person feels threatened or apprehensive. Studies of chronically disturbed people, such as schizophrenics and criminals prone to violence, show that they require consistently larger protective envelopes; they cannot allow even an unmenacing psychiatrist to approach closer to them than a distance of three feet, while normal subjects will

Letting off the steam that boils up in traffic mishaps, two Parisian motorists fiercely contest who sideswiped whom. Such tension-filled incidents are a commonplace occurrence in cities the world over: Paris had 15,409 automobile accidents in 1974—a figure that pales beside the 134,957 that were reported in the city of New York that same year.

Few city dwellers long escape the threat of riot—even in normally law-abiding Tokyo. At right, a 1967 student demonstration against the Vietnam War erupts into violence. The club-swinging crowd surges toward a unit of riot police, who, wearing plastic helmets and carrying aluminum shields, further protect themselves from flying rocks by massing behind huge fish nets.

let him approach half again as close before becoming uncomfortable.

Concepts of personal space vary so widely among different people in different cultures and situations that the connection between stress and urban crowding remains puzzling. How difficult it is to relate John Calhoun's Norway rats and their behavioral sinks to a city inhabited by men and women is indicated by conditions in Hong Kong. This city is considered to be the most crowded in the world. High-density areas in American or European cities seldom exceed 450 persons per acre; in Hong Kong, some tenement districts have 2,000 persons per acre. Hong Kong's disease rates—except for tuberculosis—are relatively low, its mortality rates are less than two thirds those of the United States, and its hospitalization rate for mental illness less than 10 per cent that of America. The serious crime rate comes to less than half that of America, with only one sixth as many murders and manslaughters.

Such figures intrigue and perplex many Westerners. In Hong Kong, lack of space as such is apparently not perceived as a stressful situation; when larger housing units were made available to some families, many of them promptly sublet the additional space to other people. The ability of the city's inhabitants to adapt to extreme crowding, according to sociologists, may stem from long exposure to crowding, strengthened by the patriarchal structure of Chinese families, in which tradition requires several generations to live in harmony under the same roof.

A similar phenomenon can be observed in Tokyo, where the population density is not far behind Hong Kong's, yet where antisocial behavior in everyday life is also relatively rare. Some psychologists argue that the well-known politeness of the Japanese is particularly suited to a crowded country simply as a survival device. Others have been struck by the fact that Tokyo is not so much a city as a collection of lively neighborhoods, an urban agglomeration of towns and villages with a fair degree of autonomy, each district retaining strong links to the rural place from which most of its inhabitants originally came.

Both the adaptability of the Japanese to city living and the limits of that adaptability have been noted in the Tokyo transit system. The trains are as crowded as those of any other city, perhaps more so. At one time some passengers boarded the cars wearing special "slick" coats, woven of a slippery nylon, so that they could slither more efficiently through the packed hordes. But even the most hardened commuter can endure just so much; in 1973, when conditions reached an excruciating climax, a mass rebellion of commuters took place. The revolt was triggered by a slowdown of Japan's National Railway Union, an action that clogged suburban lines carrying 10 million commuters to and from Tokyo. One morning at Ageo, 25 miles from the city, an inbound train pulled in, hopelessly late and packed to the doors—and 10,000 maddened commuters pulled the motorman from his cab, smashed the car windows and kicked in vending machines on the station platform. "Now they will know," shouted one of the mob's leaders, "we are not cattle!"

Not far behind crowding as a potential source of stress in modern living is its frequent concomitant, noise. Henry Thoreau once said that the mass of men lead lives of quiet desperation. He might have revised the phrase if he had lived long enough to spend much time in modern Singapore, Chicago or Paris. The roar of traffic and the honking of horns, the clamor of machines in factory, home and office, the blasting and hammering along city streets as old buildings are replaced by ever newer ones—the spectrum of continuous urban sounds seems to generate stresses that in many ways are as severe as those of crowding.

While human reactions to noise generally resemble those to crowding, there is one important difference. The ill effects of noise are not ambiguous or controversial: Noise erodes hearing and blocks desired behavior in many ways, often subtle. David Glass and Jerome Singer found that noise can have serious effects on humans even after it has stopped. Most people perform ordinary tasks about as well in a noisy office as in a quiet one; they may not like the sound level, but they learn to concentrate on the business at hand. However, the body reacts to noise, whether the mind blocks it or not. When the psychologists tested their subjects' galvanic skin response—a standard physiological indicator of stress based on the fact that increased surface perspiration, a symptom of stress, increases the electrical conductivity of the skin—they found that measurable amounts of stress occurred every time a tape was played, whether the noise was loud or soft, predictable or unpredictable. When this experiment was run for a half hour or more, significant patterns emerged. After four or five minutes the skin response ceased—but then the subjects and a control group were asked to solve puzzles, including some that had no solutions, and to proofread passages containing errors. Subjects exposed to any noise at all had markedly lower scores and less tolerance of frustration than those working in quiet. And in these extended-noise experiments, unpredictable noise produced more detrimental aftereffects than predictable noise; soft unpredictable noise, in fact, was worse than loud predictable noise.

To pursue the cumulative effects of noise, Glass's team studied the effect of noise on learning in families living in a 32-story apartment built over a 12-lane expressway in New York City (overleaf). This express-

A high-rise learning problem

How does noise affect learning? Psychologists discovered an unparalleled opportunity to find out in this apartment complex straddling a busy 12-lane expressway in New York City. When children who had lived in the complex four years or more were studied, those who lived on the lower—and noisier—floors proved to be at a disadvantage in discriminating between words. They scored below average on tests that required them to recognize the difference between similar-sounding words like "gear" and "beer," "cope" and "coke," and "guile" and "dial"—a key skill in learning to read.

When reading progress was checked, the results were even more striking. The children from upper floors tested in the 85th percentile, meaning only 15 per cent of all children in the United States read better; those from lower floors placed only in the 51st percentile, meaning that almost half of all American children could read better.

READING
(Percentile)

85

67

63

51

AVERAGE NUMBER OF WORD

23.0

22.0

PAIRS HEARD CORRECTLY

FLOORS

NOISE LEVEL
(Decibels)

25.8

24.9

32

26

25

19

18

12

11

5

57

60

63

66

The relationship between noise pollution, hearing, and reading ability is shown by graphs at left. Figures to the right of the building show the average noise level, measured in decibels, for groups of seven floors. The line graph over the apartments indicates the average number of like-sounding words (out of 30 pairs) distinguished by children in each seven-floor group. The pie charts record the children's reading skill by percentiles —the higher the score the better.

Bridge
ONLY

Bridge
9A H Hudson
Parkway

way—a sunken, heavily traveled concrete trench that echoed with the sounds of cars and trucks 24 hours a day—might almost have been designed as a noise-producing apparatus. And after four years or more of exposure to this noise, children living on the lower floors of the building showed significant impairment in their ability to learn to read. The message seemed all too clear: noise pollution affects humans more than they realize; the children, making a subconscious effort to filter out the expressway noise, had also screened out distinctions important to learning. Like other urbanites coping with high levels of stress, they had displayed adaptability—but, in their case, too much of it.

The case against noise as an insidious source of stress has steadily grown more serious and incontrovertible. Studies in Europe and the United States showed that industrial workers exposed to constant high sound levels suffer permanent hearing loss. In addition, the evidence increasingly links noise with stress-induced disease. Data collected at two German factories, one with a high noise level, the other relatively less noisy, revealed a higher percentage of heart, circulatory and equilibrium-disturbance problems among employees working in the noisier setting; studies in the Soviet Union indicated that workers in noisy industries have a higher-than-normal incidence of digestive and circulatory troubles; X-rays of Italian workers exposed to noise and vibration uncovered deterioration of the digestive tract in 65 per cent of those examined. The U.S. Environmental Protection Administration cited other research to indict high noise levels for detrimental effects on job performance, accident rates and absenteeism—especially when the noise was intermittent, unexpected or uncontrollable; and the World Health Organization estimated that illness and impairment due to noise may cost the world's industries four billion dollars a year. The overall cost of noise in the world outside the factory—a cost measured in frayed nerves, in loss of sleep and in the physical and mental problems that stem from such causes—is incalculably greater.

People's perceptions of noise, as of congestion, depend on context. A spectator who revels in the deafening roar of a motorcycle rally or an automobile race may be tortured by the barely audible drip of a leaky faucet in the night. A busy executive trying to concentrate on figures may be intensely annoyed by the sound of a typewriter; moreover, he is more likely to be irritated if the typewriter is being operated by someone else's secretary. Almost everyone warms to the sounds of children shouting happily in a schoolyard; when the same group troops into the hushed rooms of a library, older readers there may wince.

Sounds seem noisiest—are most unwanted, most interfering—when they are unpredictable and inappropriate. Thus the sounds annoying to city dwellers are not generally those of the office, store or factory; in such public places, one expects a certain amount of noise. It is the noise that penetrates the last crumbling bastion of privacy in a crowded world, the home, that imposes the greatest stress. And while the sources of noise have been multiplying and growing louder, as any veteran of apartment or row-house living can testify, rooms have been getting smaller, the walls and ceilings thinner.

One poignant account of the sounds of communal life comes from a study of 90 English families living on Braydon Road near Coventry, in a group of attached prefabricated housing units made, as an experiment in mass-production economy, of steel, one of the most effective sound-conducting and resonant materials known to man. "It's noises from *other* people that distress us," one resident reported to the investigators, her stiff upper lip trembling despite herself. "It's terrible, you can hear *everything*. When I clean my mirror it bangs against the wall, and my neighbor, she knocks back." A few residents seemed to enjoy the communal sound. They commented that the situation made for a certain feeling of companionship; it was possible to entertain the lady next door right through the party wall by playing her "favorite records with the gramophone turned too loud," or to invite her for tea or even to tend her child for a bit while she went shopping. But the large majority found the noise intolerable. They were driven to distraction by babies crying at night, sounds of coughing, shoes dropped at bedtime, Welsh husbands singing along with the radio and a prodigious amount of laughing and loud talk. Several interviewees indignantly reported that they could not help overhearing intimate conversations, such as a man in bed telling his wife her feet were cold (the fact that the unwilling eavesdroppers often could not hear all of these exchanges seemed to be equally annoying).

Many Braydon Road families coped with the situation in positive ways, partly by discussing common problems and solutions with neighbors and partly by taking action: curbing their children, closing their doors softly and moving the television or piano away from the wall. Of the two procedures, talk was at least as significant as action. Whether attempts at corrective measures actually reduce overall sound levels is not always as important to people as the fact that they are trying to do something about it, and in the process gain a sense of control and a feeling of relief. A survey of several hundred men and women living near the airport in Hamburg, Germany, revealed that those who suffered the constant roar of aircraft without complaining were actually more annoyed by the noise than those who had attended protest meetings or attempted (usually in vain) to insulate their windows and walls.

The feeling that something can be done about noise has as much effect on its stress as is true in the case of crowding—whether anything actually is done or not. In the experiments of David Glass and Jerome Singer, volunteers were subjected to tape recordings of various city sounds superimposed upon one another—in one case an unnerving mixture of two people speaking Spanish and another speaking Armenian, all to the chattering accompaniment of a typewriter, a desk calculator and a mimeograph machine. One group of subjects was given a task to do under the bombardment of this noise; a second group received much the same treatment but was provided with buttons that could be pressed to stop the noise and call off participation in the test. Almost all the co-

operative volunteers in the second group never used their buttons—but the fact that they knew they could use them if they had to produced startling results. Those subjects performed their tasks considerably better than their helpless neighbors. As might be expected, prediction was as important as control. In a test designed to measure the effects of predictable versus unpredictable noise, volunteers exposed to nine-second bursts of noise once a minute handled complex problems far better than those exposed to random bursts, even though the total duration of the sounds was the same.

Noise and crowding are but the most easily categorized stresses of urban life. Modern society offers many burdens ancient men never knew: the anonymity of small apartments and the loneliness of hotel rooms; the overwhelming scale of institutions, economies and nations that hover at the limits of human control; the restless, rootless quality of societies constantly changing their ideas, jobs and homes; the strain of understanding, and getting along with, strangers. To some scientists and philosophers, modern man seems to be living in a perpetual state of Condition Red, with overload approaching the danger zone and change accelerating toward an ultimate destructive spasm.

On a day-to-day basis, many inhabitants of cities have attempted to adjust to this overload the only way they know how: by tuning it out, by learning not to "get involved." Psychologist Stanley Milgram, of the City University of New York, has suggested that big-city dwellers are not rude by choice, as small-town visitors often suppose; instead, the urban dwellers may be responding to a surfeit of stimulus by turning it off inside their heads. To conserve their finite supplies of energy, the urbanites tend to keep their distance, to avoid entangling alliances and to smile less often or to be less polite to strangers. They avert eyes in elevators, give less time than they should to legitimate requests, tell people to get in touch with their secretaries or their lawyers.

Adaptation by avoidance has its limits, too. Psychologists have seen these limits in children brought up with little privacy, in stressful settings where people are always getting in one another's way. Tragically often, such children grow up restless, irritable, withdrawn and insecure. And there are quite a few faces like that in the crowd today.

Yet newcomers continue to come to the big, crowded, noisy cities. They come in a swarm of immigrants from small towns and from every corner of the earth. They come partly in spite of the stresses of urban life because the stresses are inseparable from its benefits. And they come partly in search of the stresses, for some of the stresses themselves are—sometimes—very desirable.

Stepping over the prone form of a stranger asleep in his doorway, a city dweller ignores the obstacle. His attitude may seem callous, even though the situation is clearly no emergency. But this aloofness is the urbanite's defensive reaction to the stress of constant demands for his attention from people he does not know. When help is required from him in an emergency, he gives it (page 48).

Seeking the nerve-jangling excitement that is a pleasurable aspect of city stress, crowds jostle their way through the noisy congestion of Tokyo's Ginza, a gaudy strip of stores, restaurants and theaters eight blocks long. This paradoxical appeal of urban stress stimulates a continued migration to cities. In Japan it is estimated that 31 per cent of the country's total population will be concentrated in Tokyo by 1985.

Cities attract people by their very glitter, their tension and challenge. They are sources of opportunity unavailable anywhere else—the places people go to see the sights, to be entertained, to learn, to try for the big brass ring. The city makes great demands and offers great rewards—the biggest jobs, the most intense delights, the widest choices between privacy and interaction, between work and play. This ever-present stimulation, for those who enjoy the city, is stress in its benign form.

Behavioral scientists have been slow to define and measure benign stress, but every city dweller has experienced it. After a year away from New York City—it might have been Paris or Tokyo or Rome —journalist Gay Talese returned with a new appreciation of the metropolis. New York, he conceded, "is ugly, it's over-programmed, over-crowded, over-neurotic and over-skilled." But, he went on to say, "it's where I think I can do my best work. It's where the most stimulating and interesting minds are. You feel the pressure of having to be at your best—and you have to be at your best in order to stay here. It's not a place for the slow-footed or slow witted. The word that most characterizes New York is 'energy,' and that's what you miss in other places." What Talese called energy a behavioral scientist might well call stress.

The city imposes the pressure of competition against a concentration of the most intelligent, the most talented, the most audacious—and in return it offers achievement, recognition, material rewards. It offers theaters, museums and a thousand unique shops—to those who make the effort to seek them out. At times, the very delights of urban society seem to arise out of stress itself. Think of a discotheque or rock concert: deafening sound; blinding spotlights or strobes trained upon the audience as well as the performers; packed, suffocating crowds. The ingredients amount to a recipe for stress overload and breakdown; the effect, paradoxically, is a communal experience, a shared enjoyment.

To some, even day-to-day crowding is an attraction in itself. There are those who revel in the tidal restlessness of commuters and workers at rush hours and lunch hours and in the throngs that fill streets at dusk for pleasure or shopping. Certainly such crowds contribute to the wonder, the gaiety, the sheer hurly-burly that makes a city great. And in a cheerful challenge to most persistent critics of modern society, the long-time student of the city, William H. Whyte, insists that: "What attracts people most in a city is other people. People are attracted to the very density they say they don't like. The physical amenities are an easy thing to come by . . . a place to sit, to eat, to girl-watch. They are the essence of the greatness of a city. And they're right under our nose."

Making it in the big town

"There's a broken heart for every light on Broadway," cautioned a popular song of 1915. But that admonition is ignored every year by thousands of youngsters who, like Nancy Reynolds *(right, foreground)*, leave home for that maelstrom of urban stress, New York City. They gladly take on the pressures of noise, crowding, insecurity and loneliness in a quest for success and sophistication. If all do not become rich and famous, most, like Nancy, adapt to the negative stresses and enjoy the positive ones.

For 23-year-old Nancy, who aspired to a career as an actress, the metropolis demanded drastic changes. Raised on a ranch outside Tulsa, Oklahoma, she moved into an apartment with three other young women, rode to work on roaring subways and spent hours in queues. "Often I get the feeling that I am being pressed in by people, people standing all around me, pushing and shoving," she said.

"I'll never forget that first day in New York," she recalled. "I expected to be attacked and mugged the second I stepped off the plane." During the next few weeks—while her activities were recorded by another newcomer to New York, French photographer Gilles Peress—she found little to counteract her forebodings. She had to endure a dreary time living in a residence hotel for women while searching for a job in an unemployment-ridden city. Trying to get work as an actress, she was turned away from auditions. But Nancy found a pleasant apartment, got a job in a travel agency and signed up for acting classes. And she began to enjoy the city's more pleasant stresses, in cafés, museums, concerts and the theater.

Anxious but tenacious, aspiring actress Nancy Reynolds walks down Fifth Avenue a few days after her arrival from Oklahoma—a plains-bred stranger seeking her first job in a city with a population of almost eight million.

PHOTOGRAPHED BY GILLES PERESS

Adjusting to new problems

"There's a lot more physical work here than in Tulsa," Nancy said, referring to such everyday matters as buying food, cleaning clothes and getting to her job. In New York, Nancy had to climb the stairs to her third-floor apartment several times a day, and she hiked long distances on crowded streets to laundries, subways and grocery stores.

Beyond the effort of unaccustomed activity was the tension of insecurity. Nancy frequently got lost. And she felt her first brush with street crime when a roommate's purse was stolen.

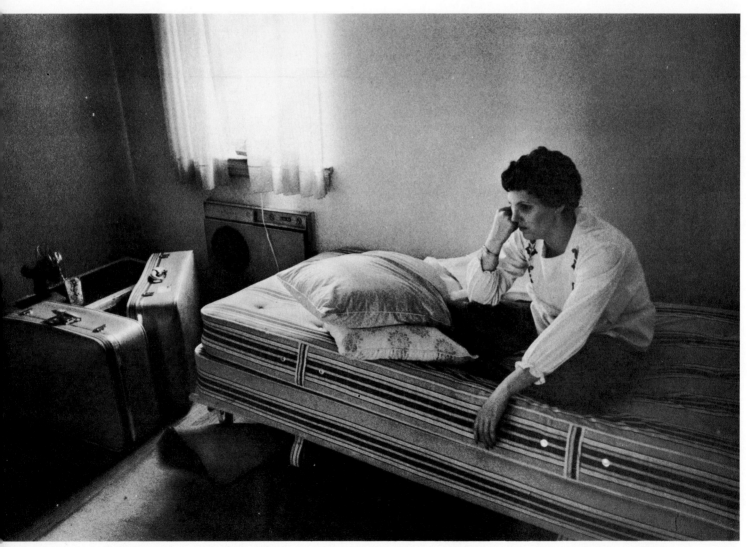

Soon after moving into an apartment, Nancy slumps in weariness on a bare bed as she contemplates the sparse furniture of her room.

Loaded with linens and clothing, Nancy causes a brief traffic jam as she asks an officer in a patrol car the way to the nearest laundry. "I had just moved into my apartment," she said, "and I knew I wouldn't sleep until the laundry was done." She added, "I don't have the greatest sense of direction"—and her photographer-companion, almost as new to the city as Nancy, could seldom help.

*Tired after a stint at a part-time job,
Nancy rides the subway. Impersonal,
often jammed and always noisy, the New
York subways proved a special stress
for Nancy, who, like most Midwesterners,
was accustomed to driving wherever
she wanted to go in her own car.*

*Nancy looks on as a police desk officer
records a complaint from one of her
roommates, whose purse had been stolen
in Central Park. Nancy was frightened at
first by reports of crime in the city, and
after her friend's experience she decided
to carry a purse as seldom as possible.
But she later took a more moderate view:
"I think that crime here is really not
as bad as people believe in the Midwest."*

Leaning against a wall for support, Nancy gives way to a moment of exhaustion after a day of job hunting. Temperatures on this midsummer afternoon hovered near 100°, the air was sticky, and the frantic pace, the crowds and the sheer difficulties of finding her way around in New York were almost too much for her. "I was so hot and tired and nauseous," she said. "I really missed home that day."

EXIT

In one of her worst moments, Nancy is refused an audition because she is not a member of the actors' union. "I thought maybe you could talk your way through," she said—but the woman at the door explained that Nancy was not eligible.

Tension is deliberately introduced to Nancy's acting classes—with lights and videotape equipment duplicating TV studio conditions. The Tulsa actress' wholesome looks led the director to cast her as a nun in her first class. But here she portrays an adulterous housewife.

In one of many job interviews during her first weeks in New York, Nancy takes a typing test at an employment agency. "I hate typing tests," Nancy said, "and the woman standing over my shoulder made me more nervous than ever."

The tough job of finding work

For Nancy Reynolds, the search for a career was doubly pressured because she had to support herself with a paying job while getting a start as an actress. Part-time work as a secretary helped cover the bills at first, and numerous, often tense interviews finally paid off when she landed a full-time job as a travel agent. But frustrating setbacks thwarted her attempts at professional acting. Turned away because she was not a member of Actors' Equity, she lamented, "I can't do anything until I get a union card."

The exhilarating compensations

Nancy nuzzles a kitten in a pet shop. "I'd love to have a cat," she said wistfully, "but it would be unfair. It would be alone so much in the city, and who would take care of it if I went on tour?"

"I was so lonely, I kept calling home," Nancy said of her early days in New York. Accustomed to a home full of pets, many friends and a number of boyfriends, she tried to ward off loneliness by dropping into pet stores to cuddle a kitten and even—at the suggestion of an acquaintance—visiting a singles bar. There, she found the atmosphere crowded and the overtures from men crude. "I hated it," she said.

But she also met new and friendly people and, taking part in the city's varied after-hours life, began to feel that she belonged in New York.

Clutching a goblet of tomato juice, Nancy perches apprehensively on a stool in a crowded singles bar (top). When a sophisticated New Yorker approached her, she laughed nervously (middle); soon afterward she was visibly enjoying the encounter (bottom). But Nancy remained cautious. When her new-found admirer suggested that he could help her start a career as a model, she dodged his request for her telephone number.

Under an early evening sky festooned with balloons, Nancy and a friend enjoy one of New York's good stresses: a picnic at a symphony concert in Central Park. Here Nancy felt the exhilaration she had hoped to find in the city's cosmopolitan atmosphere—an intense distillation of a variety of activities and people. "There was something so special about all those people gathered together," she said.

The Impact of Crisis

Above the background hum of living, with all its daily aggravations and rewards, rise occasional, unmistakable crescendos, points at which stress reaches a high pitch and demands attention in no uncertain terms. The Chinese have a word for such crisis stress that is more expressive than anything in English. They use a combination of two characters, one representing danger, the other representing opportunity. The Chinese word recognizes a strange fact about crisis stress: while it can be a brush with disaster, a potential loss, it can also be a chance for gain; oddly, it is often both things at the same time. Yet even the Chinese cannot encompass the full significance of the uncommon but uncommonly important moments of high stress. Their influence on human behavior is complex and, many scientists believe, far-reaching.

Most people think of a crisis as unexpected danger: serious illness, an accident, a fire that snuffs out a human life *(left)*. But the same physical and psychological consequences that are associated with such stress can also follow happy, long-anticipated events—promotion, purchase of a new home, birth of a child—and these occurrences, too, must be accounted as crises. The common element among these diverse crises is change, and it is the fact of drastic change, whether it is expected or unexpected, favorable or unfavorable, that makes a stress a crisis. Any kind of great alteration in the tenor of life seems to have sharp effects on behavior seemingly remote from their cause. These effects, some scientists maintain, are so pronounced that it is possible to rate crises—to assign to them their numerical values on a scale that indicates their impact and then use the scale to predict the consequences of a series of such events.

Strangest of all, the effect of crisis stress may be harmful or beneficial to an individual depending on whether he experiences it alone or with a large group of people. Communal disaster—war, a flood—can be, in some ways, good for you. Physical illnesses seem to disappear and altruism replaces selfishness. A private crisis, however, may make you sick. Rates of illness and injury appear to increase sharply. There is even evidence that death is likely to follow a severe individual crisis.

As early as the 1920s, Walter Cannon, the pioneer of modern stress research, began to record significant connections between health and critical events in the lives of individuals. In one book, Cannon cited the case of a wife in whom a thyroid disorder reached pathological proportions when "she saw her husband walking arm in arm with a strange woman and acting in such a way as to arouse jealousy and suspicion." Again, in an odd clinical study, he found that a physical disorder disappeared as soon as a stressful situation was brought to an end. The disorder was a "case of persistent vomiting which started when an income tax collector threatened punishment if a discrepancy in the tax statement was not explained." The vomiting ceased when the physician who was treating the patient "went to the collector, as a therapeutic measure, and straightened out the difficulty."

Cannon's observations were expanded and developed in the 1930s by Adolf Meyer of Johns Hopkins University. A research physician, Meyer proposed a new tool for medical diagnosis—the "life chart," which recorded both the diseases and the critical events of a patient's life and showed clear linkages between the two. In effect, the life chart represented a new kind of medical and psychological biography. "We begin with the entering of date and year of birth," Meyer wrote; "we next enter the periods of disorders of the various organs, and after this the data concerning the situations and reactions of the patient." Meyer was not only painstaking, but also profoundly original in his approach to stressful situations. He realized that an event need not be catastrophic or bizarre to have an effect upon physical and mental health; even a joyful change in the everyday pattern of life, he insisted, could do the trick. Thus, in illustrating the situations he chose for his life charts, he offered a bewildering mix of positive, neutral and negative events: "changes of habitat; of school entrance, graduations or changes, or failures; the various jobs; the dates of possibly important births and deaths in the family."

During the 1950s and 1960s Meyer's life-chart idea was refined and expanded. Eventually, the work culminated in an attempt to measure stress directly in the Social Readjustment Rating Scale *(page 91)* developed by a large group of scientists led by Thomas Holmes and Richard Rahe of the University of Washington's School of Medicine. In effect, the SRRS ranks 43 critical changes in the life of an individual according to the severity of their impact. It rates each of these changes on a scale of zero to 100 Life Change Units (LCUs).

To select the life events, assign their LCU values and test the validity of these values, Holmes and Rahe drew upon a variety of scientific techniques. To begin with, they used interviews—more than 5,000 over a period of some 20 years—and medical histories. Holmes and Rahe took the medical histories as indications of the impact of crises and tried to link them to events that had preceded illness or injury. The interviews probed for these kinds of events—negative stresses as well as positive ones such as a job promotion, the gain of a new family member, and a vacation or holiday. Because one major positive event, marriage, turned up more often in the interviews and weighed more heavily than most, they gave it an arbitrary value of 50, exactly halfway up the scale from zero to 100.

At this point they turned to the science of psychophysics, a long-established discipline for studying psychological perceptions of phenomena like pain, light and sound, and expressing these perceptions in numerical form. Psychophysics had already been used to quantify opinions and attitudes; Holmes and Rahe extended it into the field of stress. They asked some 400 men and women of varying ages, religions and marital status to compare marriage with 42 other events, all known to be stressful from clinical experience, and to assign numerical values higher or lower than 50 to these events. In each of the interviews the subject was asked such questions as these: Does the event call for more or less readjustment than marriage? Would the readjustment take longer or shorter to accomplish? The subjects themselves assigned point values according to their own evaluation of the comparative severity and duration of the readjustments, and these values formed the basis of the Rating Scale.

The Holmes-Rahe scale says much about human nature. The most severe change of all, the death of a spouse, has an LCU value of 100; the least severe, a minor infraction of the law such as a parking violation, has a value of 11. In between fall such events as divorce (73 LCUs), a marital reconciliation (45), a change of residence (20) and the rest of the 43 life events.

The fact that the death of a spouse has the greatest impact of any crisis is apparently no isolated phenomenon but an expression of a basic human characteristic. Of the 15 crises at the top of the SRRS, 10 are bound up with the family—with events such as marriage and divorce, pregnancy and the birth of a child, the death of a close family member. Only two arise from purely personal misfortunes; three deal with an individual's work.

Most scales of this kind seem to be very limited in their application; they tend to give different results in each country and culture. Not so the Holmes-Rahe scale. In the continental United States, where it was first formulated, it seemed generally applicable regardless of race or age. Minority groups such as blacks and Mexican Americans assigned much the same point values as white Anglo-Saxons; so did 13-year-old school children, showing that, as Holmes put it, a "remarkable consensus about life-change events is well established by the beginning of adolescence." Even more startling was the fact that essentially the same ratings of stress were made by people in Scandinavia, Western Europe, Spain and "a semi-literate sample from Hawaii." And the consensus continued to hold when interviews were taken in Japan, characterized

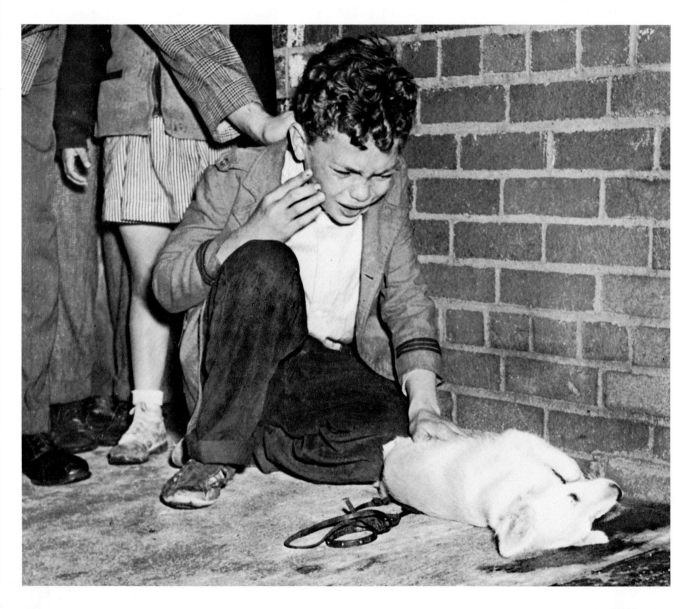

by an Oriental culture with values and social structures largely different from those of the West.

Having established their scale, Holmes and Rahe used it to see if a significant cluster of LCUs consistently led to a wide variety of disorders, physical and mental, large and small. They concluded that the LCU values are not merely arbitrary numbers; they can be combined and the combinations seem to be meaningful. In a single year, for example, a woman might marry (50 LCUs), move to a new home (20), become pregnant (40) and leave her job (26). Her LCU score for that year would come to 136—well over the scale's rating of 100 for the most severe single event, the death of a spouse. Presumably, she would be affected proportionately; the physical and psychological results of these cumulative stresses ought to be greater than those of the most extreme single crisis. Several investigations indicate that the scale does measure cumulative impact.

These studies suggest that total LCU scores might be used as an objective tool for predicting the effects of severe stress. The researchers grouped scores into categories of crisis. When events over a single year totaled 150 to 199 LCUs, an individual was said to experience a "mild" life crisis—and the medical histories of such subjects showed that 37 per cent of them underwent an appreciable change in health. After a "moderate" crisis, with an LCU score between 200 and 299, the figure rose to 51 per cent—over half of the subjects experienced health changes. And when the LCU count soared above 300, to the dimensions of a "major" crisis, no less than 79 per cent—about four out of five—fell ill within the following year.

The life changes did not have to be undesirable to do damage. Studies by Rahe of 2,500 Navy men on shipboard duty showed that both "good" and "bad" stresses seemed to be associated with subsequent illness reports. Men who had recently experienced marital or family changes of any nature went on sick call at a rate 36 per cent higher than that of those who reported no significant changes. The only category with a higher rate consisted of seamen involved in disciplinary problems: they came down with illness at a rate 44 per cent above average.

The breakdowns in health were not always severe. One study indicated that subjects with high scores suffered not only major health changes but also such minor ones as colds, cuts and bruises. The suspicion that people under stress are more accident-prone had long been raised by statistical studies of traffic accidents and deaths. It was borne out dramatically in subsequent surveys of athletes. In one such survey, made in 1969 by T. H. Holmes, 100 college football players reported

A grief-stricken 12-year-old boy weeps unbelievingly over his dog, killed in a New York street by a car just a month after it was given to him by his sister. Such emotional childhood stresses, however painful at the time, serve a long-term purpose: they prepare the individual for more severe shocks that are to come.

the life changes they had experienced during the year before the opening of the season. In accordance with their LCU scores, they were placed in groups of high, medium and low risk of injury. Three months later, at the end of the season, the researcher checked out the predictions. Studying the injury lists for all the games, he found that 9 per cent of those in the low-risk group had been hurt, 25 per cent of the medium-risk group, and 50 per cent of the high-risk group. Of the 10 athletes injured more than once during a single season, seven were among those whose LCUs had suggested high risk (in another, similar study the rate of injury in the high-risk group reached 70 per cent).

But perhaps the most astonishing evidence for the impact of a crisis on individual well-being comes from a British study bearing the appropriate code name of Broken Heart. It focused on the aftermath of the death of a man's wife. During the early 1960s Broken Heart researchers traced the lives of 4,500 widowers over the age of 54 for six months after the deaths of their wives. They expected to find—and did find—high rates of illness and depression. But they also came up with an unexpected, deeply disturbing statistic: during these six months, the subjects of the study had a mortality rate 40 per cent higher than the average for men their ages.

To account for such findings, Holmes and his colleagues proposed a simple hypothesis. They argued that the more critical the changes a person undergoes, as measured by the Rating Scale, the greater the effort he expends in adapting to them, and in the effort of adaptation he lowers his natural resistance to injury or disease. But both the Rating Scale and the theory derived from it have been attacked on several grounds. One group of critics suggests that some subjects, in order to justify severe or chronic illness, may report more disturbing life changes than others. Another insists that desirable events cannot be as taxing as unpleasant ones. The most searching criticism, however, comes from a third group of scientists, who believe that human beings are too complex and different from one another to be measured by a yardstick like the Holmes-Rahe Rating Scale. Like most attempts to relate stress to disease, it suffers from the difficulty of isolating stress from other factors such as diet, heredity and smoking and drinking habits *(Chapter 4)*. The cause-and-effect relationship between severe stress and illness, these critics point out, may be more apparent than real—just as yellow fever was believed to be caused by swamp air until 1900 when Walter Reed proved that the cause was not the swamps themselves but a virus spread by mosquitoes bred in the swamps. To the adherents of this school, an individual's health is affected not by a series of discrete events but by all

An Italian father breaks down and cries uncontrollably while escorting his daughter to the altar on her wedding day. Although weddings are supposed to be happy events, the emotional stress frequently reduces the participants, friends and relatives to tears, and here even the bride herself seems upset.

the factors of his relationship with his environment and his society.

One investigator who explored the influence of environmental and social factors was neurologist Harold Wolff of New York City's Cornell University Medical College. Wolff believed that the objective magnitude of a crisis did not count so much as whether the individual saw it as a crisis, something threatening his self-esteem or his ability to cope. Accordingly, he formulated his own theory to account for varying responses to critical stress. He wrote: "Man's attempts to adapt to life situations which do not fulfill his needs, which frustrate his aspirations, or which place heavy and conflicting demands upon him are very often associated with an increased susceptibility to all forms of illness." So far, his theory agreed with that of Holmes and Rahe. But he added: "In the population in general, those who are having difficulty in adapting to challenging life situations are those who exhibit a major proportion of the illnesses."

In long-term studies of thousands of telephone company employees in New York City, Wolff and his colleague, Dr. Lawrence E. Hinkle Jr., found a significant difference between chronically ill telephone operators and those who were free of illness. The first group consisted largely of women who considered themselves stuck in the wrong jobs; these women lived in a sort of perpetual state of crisis, and their poor health reflected that fact of their lives. The telephone operators least subject to sickness were women whose backgrounds, aspirations and interests more closely matched the circumstances in which they found themselves—that is, women who had what industrial psychologists call a good "job-personality fit."

Most of these healthy workers were women of lower middle-class backgrounds with elementary-school educations. They were generally content with their lot in life, regarded their work as satisfying and not too difficult, and liked their associates; their attitudes carried over into their homes, and most of them got along well with the other members of their families. In contrast, a number of the operators who were often ill turned out to be women with professional backgrounds and with a high-school or some college education. These chronically ill women tended to describe their duties as confining or boring, and they were unhappy both at work and at home. Moreover, their life histories showed that their illnesses usually occurred in "clusters" that coincided with periods of special crisis; this result might seem to confirm the Holmes-Rahe Rating Scale, but it can also be viewed as an indication of the individual's personal susceptibility to disease.

The difference between the two groups of telephone operators seemed to be, in effect, a difference of expectations. In those who were chronically ill, high stress and repeated crisis clearly had something to do with a life of unfulfilled expectations. In the others, fulfilled expectations had produced lives in which crises could be weathered and health was generally good. In fact, over a third of the healthiest subjects had endured major changes and deprivations with no apparent ill effects.

One of the healthiest and happiest of all the operators had a life history that would make a psychiatrist blanch—but her unfortunate background had led her to expect little from life, and her adaptation to the adult world was remarkably successful. The daughter of an alcoholic longshoreman and a teen-age girl, this woman grew up in an atmosphere of poverty and constant squabbling, punctuated by the deaths of four of her nine brothers and sisters. When she was three years old her father deserted the family; when she was five her mother was judged unfit to raise her, and she spent the next eight years in a series of orphanages. At the age of 13 she was put to work as a domestic servant, but three years later she embarked upon a series of other jobs and casual love affairs carried on, as she put it, "all over town." Then, at 23, she went to work for the telephone company, and at 27 she married a plumber's helper who was neurotic, chronically sick and usually out of work. They had no children, and when she was 44 he died in her arms; at the time she was interviewed she had been a widow for 10 years. How had the crises of her life affected this woman of low expectations? The researchers found that she was one of the most stable, highly respected and well-liked of all the company's employees. The only illness she had suffered during her 31 years as a telephone operator consisted of a few common colds—though she did admit to a spell of "nervousness" after her husband's death.

In investigations of other workers, and of refugees from Communist

A dejected man slumps idly at a London unemployment-insurance office, victim of one of the most severe of all personal stresses in an industrialized world; losing a job not only brings economic uncertainty, but also undermines the individual's sense of dignity and identity as an independent breadwinner.

China and Hungary who were adjusting to a new life in the United States, the Cornell team was impressed again and again by a phenomenon they called emotional insulation. The term refers to a kind of psychological immunity to the unsettling elements in people's lives or surroundings, and a corresponding ability to endure crises and hardships that often overcome more vulnerable types. Hinkle, who studied the phenomenon most closely, concluded that some people are less susceptible than others to the upsets of change because they interpret their environment as less threatening, challenging or demanding. Job frustrations, separation from family or country, the loss of a husband or wife —in the long run these individuals take all such adversities in stride.

Hinkle found that his emotionally insulated, stress-resistant subjects had certain personality traits in common. They were unusually flexible in their attachments to other people, groups and goals, and readily shifted to other relationships when established ones were disrupted. Many displayed a clear awareness of their own psychological limitations. If such a person saw it as his lot in life to work at an undemanding job, to live alone, to fail to get ahead, he felt no need to be unhappy about it, or to rebel.

In study after study, the same pattern emerged. "The anthropologists, psychiatrists, psychologists, sociologists and physicians who were involved in our various studies," Hinkle said, "were very different, yet they all commented on the fact that the healthiest members of our samples often showed little psychological reaction to events and situations which caused profound reactions in other members of the group."

Relatively few people are—or would want to be—so armored against emotional involvement that they resist stress as completely as did the "healthiest" subjects in Hinkle's studies. But the variation in impact of severe stress appears wide. It depends not only on the personality of the individual but also on a number of factors that are related to the stressful event. One influence seems to be knowledge—an understanding of what is happening.

Realistic and believable information—ideally, in advance of a crisis —is believed to help mitigate shock and adverse aftereffects. The information can consist of nothing more than a warning signal, as demonstrated in many laboratory experiments. At New York's Rockefeller University, for example, psychologist Jay Weiss and his colleagues subjected caged rats to mild electric shocks. Some rats heard a beeping tone that began exactly 10 seconds before each shock; others also heard the tone, but at random intervals unrelated to the timing of the shocks. Both groups of rats were subject to stress; both developed stomach ul-

For these Cretan widows, as for all adults, the death of a spouse is life's greatest stress.

Social Readjustment Rating Scale

Rank	Life event	LCU value
1.	Death of spouse	100
2.	Divorce	73
3.	Marital separation	65
4.	Jail term	63
5.	Death of close family member	63
6.	Personal injury or illness	53
7.	Marriage	50
8.	Fired from job	47
9.	Marital reconciliation	45
10.	Retirement	45
11.	Change in health of family member	44
12.	Pregnancy	40
13.	Sex difficulties	39
14.	Gain of new family member	39
15.	Business readjustment	39
16.	Change in financial state	38
17.	Death of close friend	37
18.	Change to different line of work	36
19.	Change in number of arguments with spouse	35
20.	Mortgage over $10,000	31
21.	Foreclosure of mortgage or loan	30
22.	Change in responsibilities at work	29
23.	Son or daughter leaving home	29
24.	Trouble with in-laws	29
25.	Outstanding personal achievement	28
26.	Wife begins or stops work	26
27.	Begin or end school	26
28.	Change in living conditions	25
29.	Revision of personal habits	24
30.	Trouble with boss	23
31.	Change in work hours or conditions	20
32.	Change in residence	20
33.	Change in schools	20
34.	Change in recreation	19
35.	Change in church activities	19
36.	Change in social activities	18
37.	Mortgage or loan less than $10,000	17
38.	Change in sleeping habits	16
39.	Change in number of family get-togethers	15
40.	Change in eating habits	15
41.	Vacation	13
42.	Christmas	12
43.	Minor violations of the law	11

A yardstick for personal stress

Although stresses affect each individual uniquely, their relative importance is remarkably uniform, as psychiatrists Thomas H. Holmes and Richard Rahe found in compiling the Social Readjustment Rating Scale *(right)*. But some surprises turn up in its ranking of the impact of 43 common experiences on a numerical scale of Life Change Units. For example, the death of a close friend, usually considered extremely stressful, ranks well below such events as retirement or an illness in the family. On the other hand, certain joyful events, such as a marriage or a marital reconciliation, prove to be far more stressful than financial catastrophes like bankruptcy or the foreclosure of a mortgage.

While 5,000 subjects in Europe, the United States, Central America, Oceania and Japan agreed generally upon the ranking of the 43 stressful events, differences between cultures did appear. Among the punctilious Japanese, minor violations of the law did not rank at the bottom of the scale but near the middle, and an actual jail sentence ranked second on their stress list.

Special circumstances within a culture also had an effect. For interviews of college athletes, the scale omitted such events as pregnancy and retirement, substituting others with surprisingly high LCU values; among them were "Being dropped from the team" (LCU value, 52) and "Troubles with the head coach" (35 LCUs). But in all groups, everywhere, the scale proved to have a grim usefulness as a tool for predicting stress-related illness: the higher an annual LCU score, the greater the likelihood of such illness.

cers in the course of the experiment. But the rats that could predict the timing of the shocks developed relatively few gastric ulcers; those that received identical shocks without reliable warning signals had gastric lesions almost six times as severe.

In a series of related experiments, pairs of rats were given identical shocks and warning signals. Then one member of each pair was taught to leap onto a platform or touch a special panel when the signal sounded; pressure against the platform or the panel broke the electrical circuit and prevented both rats from being shocked. In the course of the experiments the rats that controlled the situation by cutting off the torment developed considerably fewer ulcers than their helpless team mates and lost less than half as much body weight. Like human subjects who could predict and control loud bursts of objectionable noise *(pages 64-65)*, the rats armed with information about an imminent stress took the stress better, and the ability to do something about it made the threat of stress easier to bear.

The importance of a warning—and the stress of events that come without one—are familiar enough in human life. People often plan events for their shock value to get a special effect or to drive a point home. A group stages a surprise party for a friend, then gleefully springs it on him, watching his initial reaction of alarm, his wide-eyed effort to grasp what is going on, and finally his outburst of nervous laughter. In less playful circumstances, people speak resentfully of unexpected bad news coming as a "bolt out of the blue," and look less kindly on the messenger who brings it.

When an imminent situation or event is certain to be severely stressful, a doctor, counselor or parent usually tries to give the person involved some advance notice—something to worry about ahead of time, so that the blow will be less upsetting when it comes. This form of deliberate stress acts as a sort of psychological inoculation, not unlike its medical counterpart; it gives the patient a mild case of the disease beforehand in order to build up his resistance to the real thing. Getting someone to think about and prepare for a situation in advance is useful at many levels. It relieves the pain of a dentist's drill when the dentist warns "this may hurt a little." The pangs of a first childbirth are generally eased if the mother knows what to expect and what she can do to help. And the same kind of foreknowledge is useful in coping with the realities of a major illness.

The value of what Yale University psychiatrist Irving Janis calls the work of worrying was vividly illustrated when Janis interviewed patients undergoing major surgery before and after their operations. The patients who worried least ahead of time, he discovered, were the ones who suffered most after the fact. During routine preoperative care in the hospital, these patients remained generally calm, slept well, adopted a jaunty "there's-really-nothing-to-it" attitude and made little effort to gather information about the operation and its possible aftereffects. Then, when the anesthetic wore off, they suddenly found themselves contending with more pain and inconvenience than they had ever anticipated. Most of them reacted with resentment, anxiety and depression. Many sank into prolonged moods of grouchiness, punctuated by belligerent outbursts, refusals to conform with postoperative procedures, even charges that the hospital staff was negligent, incompetent or downright sadistic. Long after their convalescence, these patients looked back upon their operations as unnecessarily disturbing experiences, and they tended to blame their woes on the medical profession in general.

Curiously, the patients who experienced very high levels of fear before their operations were only slightly better off. Jittery and nervous in anticipation of the surgeon's knife and given to spells of insomnia and weeping, some attempted to postpone or cancel their surgery or even left the hospital against medical advice. During convalescence, most were still concerned that they might not fully recover. And though these high-level worriers were grateful to their nurses and doctors, and tried to follow postoperative orders, their susceptibility to fear and their need for reassurance remained high.

It was the patients with a moderate degree of anticipatory fear who made the best adjustment to postoperative stress, Janis found. They had generally asked for information about the impending surgery, and even during occasional periods of fretfulness they rehearsed the anticipated discomforts in their minds. After surgery, when they were subjected to just as much physical discomfort as their disgruntled or nervous brethren, these part-time worriers, as Janis called them, showed remarkably few symptoms of emotional disturbance and were generally regarded as model patients by the staff. Clearly, in this middle range of personality types, the right amount of psychological inoculation and realistic fear built resistance to stress and helped counteract its effects.

The foreknowledge that seems to mitigate personal stress also seems to lessen group crises that strike entire communities and societies. If a town is given sufficient warning of an impending flood, for example, it may be able to take appropriate steps to prevent damage and thus forestall a crisis. This similarity between individual and group crises is less striking, however, than the differences. For in most respects,

Scrambling over one another, spectators at a soccer match flee fire in a Turkish stadium. But panic did not overwhelm everyone—some people (upper and lower right) paused to survey the situation. Panic turned out to be unnecessary—the fire, in a snack bar, proved minor—but 68 people were injured in the crush.

severe stress takes on an entirely new character when it affects whole groups of people together.

Natural and man-made disasters—fires and floods, tornadoes and hurricanes, epidemics and wars—provide unique laboratories for observing both individuals and social systems. In such group crises, events are intensified and compressed into concrete time spans, large masses of people confront the same challenges, and behavior that is normally private becomes plain for all to see. And the major finding about this behavior is a surprising one. Large-scale catastrophes can and do take a toll in physical and psychiatric suffering and in death. But the evidence suggests that most people and institutions come through such ordeals largely intact—indeed, perhaps even stronger and better integrated than they were before.

People react differently to collective crises, of course. For many, the first tendency is an instinctive denial that a crisis exists at all. Warned of an oncoming flood or an enemy bombing attack, the inhabitants of whole towns have ignored the information or have persisted in misinterpreting danger signals as normal phenomena until too late.

Charles E. Fritz of the American National Research Council has classified such misinterpretations in a variety of disasters. According to him, people will draw false conclusions from past experiences ("The river never got higher than this before"). They will conform to the behavior of their equally unheeding neighbors ("Nobody else seems to be doing anything about it"). They will even misread their own perceptions ("It looks like just another bad storm"). A man trying to sleep while a flood swept through Canvey Island, England, reported: "I woke up and heard what I thought was the rain dripping down the chimney. Then I reached down for my pipe and my hand went straight into the water." A far more devastating flood on the Rio Grande nearly wiped out the towns of Piedras Negras, Mexico, and Eagle Pass, Texas, killing more than a hundred people and injuring over 4,000 others. Yet at least 90 per cent of the two populations had received warning of the flood a day or more before it arrived; only a handful had left home.

When a warning must be accepted as both true and inescapable, some people resort to irrational defenses. They may attempt to ward off the danger by reassuring themselves that they do not deserve to be punished. Under the threat of air raids in World War II, civilians in Britain, Germany and Japan displayed a marked increase in religious interest and a general asceticism of behavior, as though a praiseworthy way of life would protect them. Personal attempts to control fate occasionally reached bizarre extremes: some Japanese civilians, for example, tried

Clinging upside down to a fire-swept building in Tel Aviv, an office worker is pulled to safety by coolheaded colleagues who clutch at his shoes. Their calm reaction is more common than panic. In this case it prevented a disaster. Although the building was gutted, only one of its 600 occupants was killed.

a number of odd nostrums to ward off destruction, including rubbing raw onions on their heads and wearing Western clothing, presumably to propitiate the oncoming raiders in the sky. And when planes were expected over Britain, many Londoners were seen carefully tiptoeing about as people do when trying to avoid attracting attention.

Perhaps the most notable change in the behavior of these wartime populations, however, was an understandable and probably useful jump in spontaneous communication. Exchanging jokes and war stories with virtual strangers became widespread; a large part of the normally conservative and reserved British population fell into a talkative, gregarious, business-as-usual mood that lasted through most of the war. And like others who have undergone a crisis together, many Londoners later had an odd sensation of being more fully alive during the war than at any time in their lives before or since; they recall not so much the hardships and destruction in their city as the camaraderie and the lusty singing in the bomb shelters. The British sociologist Richard Titmuss noted an "unsettling vista of smiles" among his countrymen during the Battle of Britain and was ashamed to think that it took a war to bring it about.

The systematic study of civilian behavior under wartime stress is relatively recent. But the actions of soldiers in combat have been observed and analyzed over the centuries. To the fighting man, war presents in one miserable package a number of stresses that people everywhere instinctively seek to avoid: the torture of being cold, wet and muddy or of having to share a steaming foxhole in the jungle with swarms of malarial mosquitoes; the lack of privacy, sleep and decent food; the noise and confusion of battle; the frustration of never really knowing what is going on; the inner struggles among the demands of self-preservation, obligations to families back home and loyalty to country; and perhaps worst of all, the horror of death or maiming injury, and the enormous sense of loss when a friend who has shared all the other hardships is no longer there.

Soldiers have often collapsed under the cumulative effects of such pressures—and have been described by stiff-necked military commanders as cowards who "lack moral fiber." More and more, however, these effects have been recognized as medical and psychiatric problems, with a common cause in insupportable stress. Accuracy of diagnosis has been slow in coming. During the United States Civil War, a condition termed "nostalgia" by the Surgeon General of the Union Army afflicted thousands of soldiers, rendering them incapable of carrying out their duties even though they gave no overt signs of injury or poor health; the more severe cases were discharged on such vague grounds as "paralysis" or simply "insanity." During the First World War, men on both sides were often pinned down helplessly in trenches under relentless artillery bombardment; military doctors ascribed the dazed, incoherent behavior of many such men to physical brain damage from the concussion of high explosives, and coined the catchall term shell shock for the hypothetical ailment. In the Second World War the unexpectedly high number of psychiatric disorders were at first labeled psychoneurosis, then exhaustion, and finally combat fatigue.

To modern students of stress, the concepts of fatigue and exhaustion come closest to the mark. These concepts do, in fact, explain the results

of psychological and physical hardships that, if prolonged or severe enough, can wear any man down. General S. L. A. Marshall suggested that sustained fear by itself can sap a man's bodily energy. In July 1918, Marshall led a regiment to the front in France and saw the men around him almost collapse from fatigue after an 11-mile march—although in training the same men had carried similar packs on 20-mile marches under a hot sun. When the men's fear lifted, they lost their fatigue: marching away from the front, the troops made 32 miles in a single day "feeling light as a feather." Decades later, as an observer in World War II, Marshall saw tragic effects of fear-induced fatigue. One soldier, he reported, was so weakened that he was physically unable to crawl across a beachhead under enemy fire, though he knew that to stay where he was amounted to suicide.

Fear of one's own death is not the only mortal fear in warfare. One World War II study showed that the fear of killing another human being was the most common single cause of battle failure or combat fatigue. Most soldiers, conditioned from childhood to respect the sanctity of human life, try to avoid the grim necessity of killing as far as possible. During the Civil War, soldiers were seen to react to the strain of combat by throwing their weapons away ("Seeing what had been thrown away," said an observer after the battle of Cold Harbor, "I wondered how the battle had been fought"); and after the battle of Gettysburg, the men who collected the thousands of discarded rifles found that most of them had never been fired.

Only one thing, says Marshall, is valued more than life itself by the majority of men: personal pride and honor. All men in combat live with fear; what makes most face the risk of death is not the thought of martyrdom or a medal, but the more basic fear of losing the respect of the men fighting alongside them, of letting their buddies down.

"Social responsibility," says Peter Bourne, a psychiatrist who headed a medical research project in Vietnam, "causes much more stress in wartime than the threat of being killed." Moreover, Bourne noted, the responsibilities of decision making often produce the greatest stress of all. Officers behind the front lines often display symptoms of more severe stress than men actually under fire. The most vulnerable to the stress of responsibility are younger men with little experience, thrust into positions in which they must handle the burden of someone else's life or death. On one hospital ship leaving Vietnam, the psychiatric patients consisted almost entirely of such men—young corporals who had been promoted to squad leaders in the field, or medical corpsmen who had worked against impossible odds to stem a flood of casualties. Most

Bearing pictures of dead relatives and friends, demonstrators in the Japanese town of Minamata demand action after some 100 deaths and 700 serious injuries had been caused by mercury-bearing waste from a local industry. The victims, drawn together by the crisis, campaigned for 14 years and finally won compensation that totaled more than $80 million.

of these patients were deeply shaken by guilt feelings for the loss of men entrusted to their command or care. But even trained young officers of the lower grades suffered from high levels of stress, induced not by the threat of enemy attack, but by the tasks of reconciling rapid-fire orders from distant superiors with the realities of the forward situation, and having to prove their abilities to older and more experienced sergeants who were convinced that they were actually in control of the group.

Although many people crack under the blows of severe group stresses or react irrationally by finding all kinds of excuses for illogical responses, such behavior is much less common than supposed. In war and peace most people bear up astonishingly well in the worst of crises, despite the impressions created by bad military novels, disaster movies and sensationalized reports of collective ordeals. In some 140 catastrophies studied during a quarter of a century by the Committee on Natural Disasters of the National Academy of Sciences and the Disaster Research Center of Ohio State University, populations that were confronted with tornadoes, floods or earthquakes did not flee the scene in panic-stricken hordes, nor did armies of looters and rapists prowl the silent, shattered streets. The research found that again and again, even in the most appalling circumstances, individuals generally responded with remarkable speed, common sense and basic humanity to the urgent needs of the moment.

L ike a war, a civil disaster is high drama, a common crisis that rivets the attention of thousands or even millions of people on press reports. When an earthquake strikes, a skyscraper catches fire or a luxury liner founders in a typhoon, an enormous audience goes on alert, suffering with the victims, searching for villains and heroes, thrilling to triumphs and tragedies. In its vicarious stress-seeking, however, the audience sometimes reads into the story facts that may not actually be there. A casual observer entering a disaster area is often struck by what seems aimless, conflicting behavior: some people running, or racing in cars in different directions, others digging frantically in piles of debris, still others standing around looking dazed or talking excitedly to one another. These apparently random, unpatterned actions suggest disorganization, even panic, particularly to outsiders who come to look.

In many civil disasters, visitors compound the crisis. The job of rescue and reorganization is made more difficult by the number of outsiders who spontaneously move toward the scene, in what disaster experts call a "convergence phenomenon." Some are simply curious to see what the disaster looks like; others are anxious about friends or relatives, and many come into the area to do what they can to help. Inevitably, policemen, firemen and civil defense volunteers find their work complicated by monumental traffic jams. Two days after a tornado in White County, Arkansas, cars were still piled up bumper to bumper for 10 miles on either side of a stricken town, blocking emergency vehicles and diverting highway patrolmen needed for other tasks. Minutes after a major disaster is reported, switchboards in the affected area are overloaded with inquiries and offers to help. Not long after that, tons of unsolicited supplies begin to arrive, often creating major problems of sorting, storing and simply getting rid of the stuff. After the White County tornado an exhausted Red Cross worker summed up the volunteered materials of mercy: "About 60 per cent of it is useless—everything from high-button shoes to derby hats. Almost no work clothes, which we could have used. We did get a fancy-dress tuxedo, though, a nice one, in good condition. And a great big carton of falsies."

Such ludicrous responses to real needs are not at all typical of the people directly involved. They may seem to be acting aimlessly and inappropriately to an unaffected observer but, according to disaster expert Charles E. Fritz, what the observer is usually witnessing in such situations is not panic at all. He sees a collection of individuals and impromptu groups who are intently focused upon urgent tasks—they are looking for lost relatives or misplaced possessions, organizing spontaneous rescue missions, or studying the scene and exchanging information in attempts to understand exactly what has happened and to decide upon the next move.

The first thing almost all survivors do in a disaster, Fritz observed, is to check on the safety of family and friends; after that, a high percentage turn to see if anyone else needs help. Within a half hour after the tornado hit White County, 32 per cent of the people there were searching for missing persons, 11 per cent were rescuing victims and 35 per cent were engaged in various other acts of emergency relief. Over the next six hours almost the entire community got involved in these activities: 28 per cent in searching, 22 per cent in rescue and 46 per cent in general emergency relief. In such a collective crisis, many people find new roles and a chance to prove their worth. Teenagers, for example, who often consider their everyday roles boring and frustrating, generally pitch in with a zest that astounds their elders. And in almost all disasters, those with minor injuries are generally calm, quiet and undemanding, and often suggest that rescuers help others who may be in worse shape.

*After storming and capturing a hill under
heavy fire, U.S. Marines form a human
chain to evacuate fallen comrades
through a sea of mud in Vietnam in 1966.
Front-line warfare involves the severest
of stresses, and it often inspires
the utmost in cooperation among men.*

Throughout the community as a whole, vague tensions, commonplace worries and conflicts fade in the face of a single, recognizable challenge that people can see plainly and do something about. In the wake of a large-scale disaster, danger and suffering become common property, rather than any one individual's tough luck, and there is little time for aloofness, boredom or antagonisms. Such changes in outlook seem to be reflected in medical statistics. Chronic stress-related disorders ease off, there is a slackening of admissions to mental hospitals and psychiatric clinics and the suicide rate takes an appreciable dip. What is more, studies in town after town have shown that few verified cases of theft, looting or profiteering occur, and that the crime rate in general decreases.

Disaster-watchers in peace and war have repeatedly described a general lifting of morale in the stricken population. After the San Francisco earthquake and fire of 1906, the psychologist William James was impressed by the speed with which people improvised order out of chaos —but he was astounded by the "universal equanimity" of the survivors, and by the cheerfulness and helpfulness they exhibited. The Polish writer Dominik Wegierski, who fled from Kraków to the countryside when the Nazis bombed the city in 1941, was struck by the way his rural compatriots forgot old quarrels and opened up their hearts and homes to the refugees (even to tax collectors and policemen who in other times, Wegierski dryly noted, could hardly enter a house without being bitten by the dog).

In the aftermath of collective tragedy or near-tragedy, families almost always become more closely knit and develop stronger ties to kin and community. Somehow, danger and deprivation break down the social and psychological isolation that usually characterize the modern world. People merge in a primary, almost a tribal group, a nucleus from which the larger society will eventually be reconstituted. Observing this phenomenon, Charles Fritz wrote of a "community of survivors," which he described as "intimate, personal, informal, sympathetic, direct, spontaneous."

The phenomenon is often very large in scale. In what sociologist Robert I. Kutak called the democracy of distress, great masses of people look upon one another with fresh insight; ethnic, economic and social distinctions tend to vanish, sometimes for long after the crisis has eased. The Italian writer Ignazio Silone, speaking of a disastrous earthquake that leveled the city of Messina and killed 50,000 people in 1915, suggested a deeper human meaning of such events: "In a district like ours many injustices go unpunished. An earthquake achieves what the law promises but does not in practice maintain—the equality of all men."

The idea of a phoenix rising from the ashes of calamity has intrigued storytellers and historians for thousands of years. Because major social crises expose their participants to dramatic object lessons, speed up decision making and force new solutions, they carry with them extraordinary opportunities for advance. Often for the first time, people see that others are fundamentally like themselves—an insight that for many is tremendously revealing and heartening. This new sense of solidarity can be put to work in a kind of moral and physical rebuilding, a reaction to collective stress that some social scientists call an amplified rebound. The momentum of an amplified rebound can carry men, communities and even nations to new levels of integration and achievement. It does not always do so. A sweeping or prolonged crisis may leave a community depleted of the energies and resources needed for revival. Elsewhere, the amplified rebound may simply not occur: some historians describe Great Britain as a nation that, after a heroic rallying of spirit in World War II, entered a period of confusion and slow decline. By contrast, within 10 years after that war the Soviet Union, which had suffered 2.5 million civilian casualties, more than recouped its wartime losses in productivity and growth. In West Germany, seemingly crushed by defeat, industrial production rose to 70 per cent more than the prewar level within a decade. And in Japan, where over 65 cities had undergone saturation bombing, almost a million civilians had died and 1.3 million had been injured, the comparable production figure reached an astonishing 177 per cent.

These successes followed ordeals no society would willingly bring upon itself. But just as the disasters of the crises had been far worse than could have been anticipated, so was the aftermath more glorious. From crisis had come triumph.

Torment of a nation in chains

From 1940 to 1944 the people of France lived under Nazi military occupation that subjected them to bitter pressure of a kind rarely suffered by an entire nation for so long. And yet, severe though the stresses were, the majority of the population adapted to them.

The French entered the Occupation stunned and shamed by their army's collapse after a six-week war; two million of their young men were prisoners of war. Food shortages developed as the Nazis levied requisitions of grain and meat for their troops. Frenchmen lost the right to have radios or telephones, to send wires or to leave town without permission. Perhaps most frightening was the threat of arbitrary arrest and deportation (right), a personal disaster that seemed ever imminent.

The French reacted to the stresses in three ways. Some fought back. But the Resistance attracted fewer than 250,000 out of a 40 million population. Some Frenchmen went over to the Nazis: 32,000 became Gestapo spies. Some did neither: the surprising fact is not that there were heroes and villains, but that the majority conducted their lives much as they always had.

The French got along apparently because they followed what seems to be a general human pattern, detected in experiments conducted by Muzafer Sherif and his associates at the University of Oklahoma. They tested students' reactions to a dilemma and found that most people draw together in the face of a common problem, which increases their morale and helps them to withstand stress. The French quietly closed ranks against the invaders and, as a survivor recalls, lived "in closed circles, all sharing the one quality of prudence."

The ordinarily impassive demeanor of inhabitants of the Old Port section of Marseille gives way to stares of dismay as Nazi soldiers announce that the entire quarter is to be destroyed, a reprisal for an attack on German officers in January 1943. After the residents had been forcibly evacuated, thousands were sent to concentration camps.

When ordinary life became extraordinary

In the early stages of the Occupation, the stresses on a Frenchman could be nothing more than queues for food. Some citizens even took the food shortage as a sporting challenge. Remembers one, "The Frenchman loves to scrounge, so he had to try his luck at getting more bread than he was rationed."

But as the War dragged on, the stresses became much more drastic (*following pages*). The effect was to draw the people closer together in smaller units of solidarity, as indicated by a post-War study of the survivors of bombings, which found a strengthened cohesion of families resulting from the War.

A free soup line was one restaurant owner's defiant attempt to ease the plight of his fellow Parisians under Nazi rule. The star worn by the man in the center is his required identification as a Jew.

Ration cards (below) purchased so little food—only 900 to 1,200 daily calories—that everyone resorted to the black market, a violation of law so essential it was openly condoned by the Church.

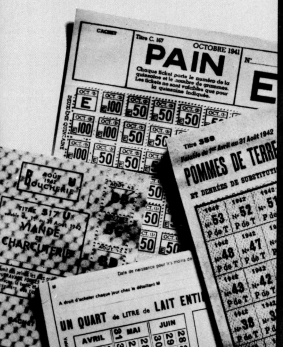

Faced with freezing temperatures in their coal-less apartments, resourceful Parisians beat the chill by cutting and hauling off branches from the city's trees.

Though these Paris youngsters are marching bravely enough to the railway station for evacuation to the safety of the countryside, such separation from parents, later studies showed, proved to be more harmful to the children than the stress of dodging bombs.

Traditional qualities of the French
farm family—thrifty neatness and courage
—sustain this group, guarding tidily
stacked belongings at a shelter during
the Allied invasion of France in 1944, and
awaiting word that they can go home.

Notices like the one at right ordered
Frenchmen to forced labor in Germany.
But some 100,000 defied the orders,
hiding out from the Occupation forces.

ÉTAT FRANÇAIS

PRÉFECTURE DE L'HÉRAULT

SERVICE
DU TRAVAIL OBLIGATOIRE
(C. M. 1 C du 21 fév...

LE PRÉFET DÉLÉGUÉ

à M. *Labour Jacques*
Rue Villefranche 33
Montpellier
(HÉRAULT)

MONSIEUR,

J'ai l'honneur de vous informer que vous avez été désigné par
la Commission compétente pour être affecté à un travail en
Allemagne.

Je vous invite à vous présenter le *Mercredi 15/9*

Neighbors in the village of St. Marcouf lead a grief-stricken woman away from her shelled home after she has suffered the ultimate stress: the death of her husband, killed in the ruins.

Blank despair stares from the faces of women uprooted from everyday life in France and interned at a prison camp. Recalls a French survivor of Buchenwald, "You didn't really think about anything, except saving your skin."

Those who gave in: the collaborators

The artificial environment of the Occupation released traits that in peacetime were kept under control—"greed . . . anti-Semitic venom . . . a taste for cruelty" were cited in journalist Milton Dank's analysis of the motives leading Frenchmen to collaborate with the Nazis. The situation offered an opportunity to pursue normally frustrated ends, and some people seized the chance.

Among the most ardent collaborators were the 30,000 members of the French militia, a volunteer auxiliary police force set up to defeat the Resistance movement *(opposite, bottom)*. But less fanatic men and women cooperated with their captors to enjoy common human pleasures *(opposite, top)* or simply because there was no other way to earn a living *(right)*.

The 100,000th French worker to take a job in German industry (left)—he finally signed up after two jobless years—gets a cool bon voyage from the economic chief of the Occupation forces before boarding the train to leave Paris.

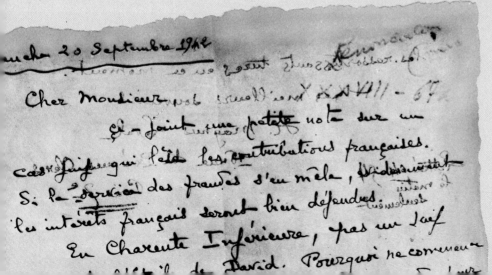

In a release of racial bigotry, a letter from an informer—one of thousands like it, some signed, some anonymous—notifies the police that a resident of Lower Charente Street is a Jew who is not wearing his identifying yellow star.

Out on the town with Nazi officers,
French girls seek a few hours' diversion
from the dreariness of wartime Paris.
Throughout the Occupation, all forms
of entertainment boomed—zoos, circuses,
movies, theater—as the French eagerly
sought relief from their prolonged stress.

A smirking member of the French militia
marches suspected Resistance fighters
through a yard in Brittany. So hated
was the fratricidal militia that membership
later became ground for execution.

Those who fought back: the Resistance

"Scientists don't fully understand what makes a man reveal unsuspected bravery under stress," said Russell Dynes of Ohio State University's Disaster Research Center, "but we do know that his bravery was latent in his character all the time—he just never had the chance to use it." Dynes's conclusion applies to many people who fought the enemy, but it precisely fits the hero of the Resistance, Jean Moulin.

Moulin was a gentle bureaucrat—the prefect of Chartres. When the Nazis came, he began uniting underground groups into a nationwide Resistance. It took him one hazardous year. A month later he was betrayed and arrested. He died under torture, silent to the end.

Laboring over a basement press, a Resistance worker prints an underground paper. Although risk of arrest was increased by photographs like this and the one below it, showing actual operations, many Resistance members were so aware of the significance of their mission they welcomed the recording of it.

A young woman tucks pistols under her baby's coverlet in a Resistance weapons-smuggling operation. Women were often gunrunners and couriers, for standard feminine gear—prams, grocery bags, handbags—enabled them to carry everything from underground newspapers to hand grenades without detection.

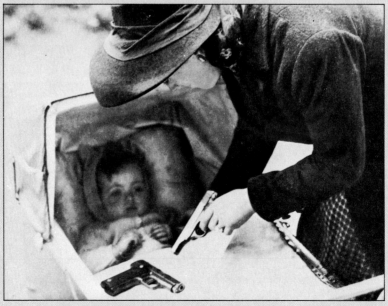

Resistance papers like the one below, published at great hazard, disseminated a spirit of opposition among the French people. "Our aim was to create a certain psychological climate around the Germans," said the editor of one.

Stationed against the corner of a building so that the bullets aimed at him will not ricochet toward his executioners, a Resistance fighter smiles at them.

25 Décembre 19

2ᵉ Année — Nº 20

Le Nouveau Journal de Paris

RÉSISTANCE

Le Nouveau Jou de Paris

APRÈS LES CONFÉRENCE DE TÉHÉRAN ET DU CAIRE

Vers la Victoire

La Guerre continue

événements d'importance pri- | Ménilmontant ou du mineur du Donets.
en | Pas de tutelles avouées ou hypocrites

Sur le front russe les batailles conti-
nuent violentes et acharnées. On peut
distinguer trois secteurs principaux
d'opérations. Entre les voies ferrées Smo-
lensk-Minsk et Gomel-Brest-Litovsk, les

mètres d'altitude. Cette partie d
me des Abruzzes est particuli
aride et tourmentée. Les lignes
tes ne sont pas toujours orient
le même sens. Rares sont le
pénétration. C'est la raison pou

The explosive release of liberation

The end of the Occupation brought a reaction in line with disaster expert Charles E. Fritz's finding that profoundly stressful situations "provide a medium for the build-up and release of emotions." After the sharing of danger and deprivation came a group explosion of contrasting feelings. One was euphoria, which sparked celebrations *(right)* as Allied troops moved in. The other was rage at traitors. A citizen of Clermont recalls, "In the three or four days following the liberation, perhaps 1,200 people were arrested, of whom only 600 reached prison. You can imagine what happened to the other 600."

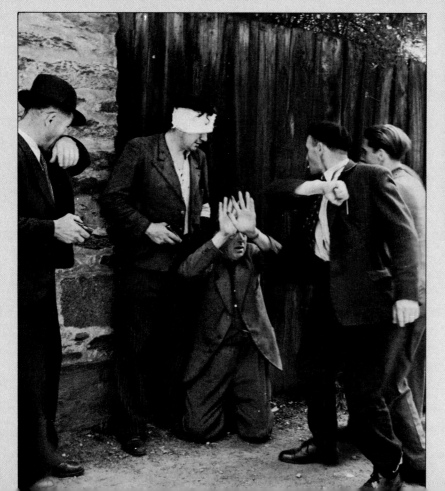

Vengeance against a collaborationist erupts in Rennes as a townsman swings a violent blow at the arrested man, one of three being held. Their captors, wrote a witness, "pushed one of the terrified wretches against a fence, smashed another's nose until blood covered his face and started in on the third."

An exuberant throng in the newly
liberated town of Isigny mobs General
Charles de Gaulle, who as wartime leader
of the Free French movement had
symbolized the nation's refusal to accept
defeat. As de Gaulle moved north to Paris
with conquering Allied forces, crowds
cheered, tossed flowers, climbed aboard
vehicles and hugged the soldiers.

117

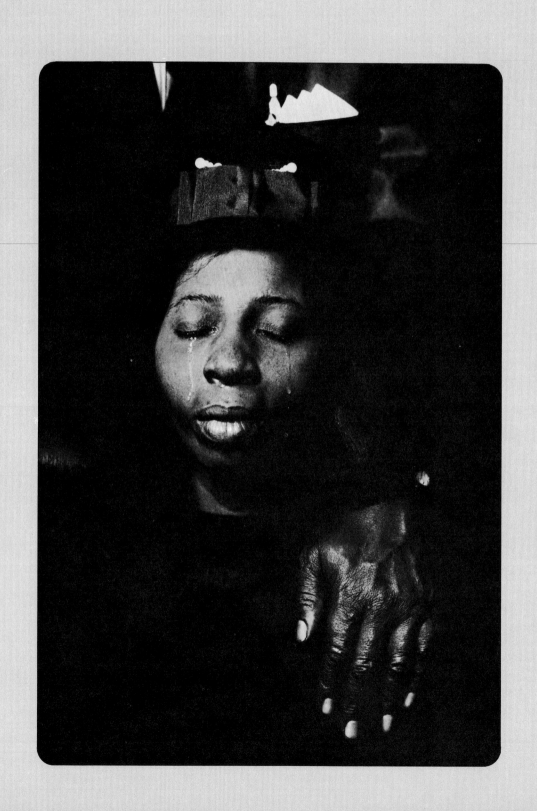

How the Body Responds

It is easier to identify the physical effects of psychological stress than to explain them. A mother weeps *(left)* over the loss of a soldier son killed in war. Children laugh at the exhilaration of play. A man frowns from the stress of annoyance. Exactly why sorrow should bring tears, and joy laughter, no one knows, although there are intriguing speculations. Equally strange are the cause-and-effect relationships between stress and physical illness. Stress—and stress alone—can in certain cases cause vertigo, blindness and even death. It is known to bring on certain types of bodily aches, ulcers and circulatory ailments, and it seems deeply implicated in many other serious diseases.

The most remarkable of the direct physical consequences of stress is death. Extreme stress, deliberately applied, is used for ritual executions in places as far apart as Australia, Borneo, central Africa and the islands of the Caribbean Sea. Anthropologists call the practice voodoo, bone-pointing or pouri-pouri, depending on the particular tribal society in which it occurs, but its horrifying course is always much the same. It is extreme punishment for the breaking of a sacred taboo. A witch doctor or medicine man points a magic bone or stick at the transgressor or simply recites fateful incantations; in either case, the ritual places the victim under a spell of death. And in emotional agony or tranquil resignation, death does come, usually in a matter of days.

That pioneer student of stress, the Harvard physiologist Walter Cannon, was fascinated by tales of such events. Skeptical at first, he checked one account after another and eventually confirmed the reports of some 30 voodoo deaths. In one of his studies, Cannon quoted a vivid description of a bone-pointing death among Australian tribesmen written by the geologist-explorer Herbert Basedow, who served as Chief Protector of Aborigines in the Northern Territory.

"The man who discovers that he is being 'boned' is a pitiable sight. He stands aghast, with his eyes staring at the treacherous pointer, and with his hands lifted as though to ward off the lethal medium, which he imagines is pouring into his body. His cheeks blanch and his eyes become glassy and the expression of his face becomes horribly distorted. He attempts to shriek but usually the sound chokes in his throat, and all that one might see is froth at his mouth. His body begins to tremble and the muscles twist involuntarily. He sways backwards and falls to the ground, and after a short time appears to be in a swoon; but soon after he writhes as if in mortal agony, and, covering his face with his hands, begins to moan. After a while he becomes very composed and crawls to his wurley [hut]. From this time onwards he sickens and frets, refusing to eat and keeping aloof from the daily affairs of the tribe. Unless help is forthcoming in the shape of a countercharm administered by the hands of the Nangarri, or medicine man, his death is only a matter of a comparatively short time."

In analyzing such deaths by suggestion, Cannon emphasized one factor in the victim's disintegration: the withdrawal of tribal support. Once the bone is pointed, the victim is immediately given up for dead by his fellow villagers; his social life collapses and he finds himself isolated in a situation from which the only escape is death. In some societies the tribe first withdraws, then returns to the victim and celebrates the rite of mourning, suggesting that he is as good as dead. In his shame and terror he may hide in his hut or in the forest, and refuse to eat or drink; but Cannon concluded that while the lack of food and fluids may weaken him physically, what actually kills him is emotional and physical shock. In effect, his nervous system is subjected to an intolerable overload of stress. His heart, exhausted by overstimulation, develops arrhythmia, a condition in which it quivers but does not pulse or beat; blood pressure drops disastrously and vital functions cease. The victim believes firmly that he is meant to die, and he simply sits in trembling fear or resignation until he finally does.

While such extreme responses to stress are the little-known exceptions in this world, the body's everyday responses are obvious to all, everywhere. When human beings are displeased, the muscles of their faces knot up in a scowl; when they are bored, they yawn; when they hear a joke they like, the muscles of the diaphragm contract to produce the staccato exhalations called laughter; when oppressed by sadness, they let out a sigh and perhaps shed a tear. Each of these reactions is an answer to stress, to a stimulus that disturbs the inner balance, and it sets in motion physiological actions that attempt to relieve tension and restore equilibrium.

Many such responses stem from primal reactions to anger or fear. A terrifying sight causes the contraction of the skin into little bumps of

As it leaps from a leopard, a baboon displays appropriate responses to ultimate stress—a threat to life. It prepares to fight as it bares menacing canine teeth and raises hair in its pelt, an automatic reaction that makes it look bigger. Within its body it prepares for both flight and injury: muscles tense, the heart pounds and blood empties from the vulnerable blood vessels near the skin.

goose flesh—a throwback to animal ancestors that stiffened fur or feathers to make them look larger and more formidable to their adversaries. Fear, even in such mild forms as anxiety or apprehension, overrules the instinct to eat; a vital survival mechanism in animals endangered by predators, this response to fear manifests itself in human beings as "butterflies in the stomach," a decrease in salivation that makes mouths go dry and leaves a bad taste, a contraction of the esophagus that produces "a lump in the throat" or makes a person choke with fright. So programed are humans by their evolutionary inheritance that extreme fear may lead to a sudden case of diarrhea—according to some scientists, a weight-lightening advantage for a deer or baboon outrunning a leopard, but hardly a convenience for an after-dinner speaker approaching the rostrum or a football player about to take the field. And a man who decides to stand and fight reveals his heritage too: the snarl of the dog is the angry sneer of the man; in both, the same type of muscle pulls back the lip to reveal a pointed canine tooth.

Even when the thinking brain tries to suppress these instinctive reactions, attempting to conceal stress, it may be overridden by other brain circuits responding to stress, so that the body inadvertently tells the truth. When a child blandly denies raiding the cookie jar, his mother knows to look for the artificiality of his innocent smile or a slight widening of his eyes when the cookie jar is mentioned.

At a deeper level, a person who makes an outwardly successful effort to conceal his emotions is often betrayed by inner signs of the stress response. In ancient China, police interrogators separated the guilty from the innocent by forcing all the suspects to fill their mouths with dry, cooked rice; according to traditional—and well-founded—lore, the culprit would be unable to moisten his mouthful with saliva and swallow it down. In the modern world the polygraph, or lie detector, does the same job in a somewhat more scientific way, by measuring involuntary physiological reactions to stress: a subject's rise and fall in pulse rate, blood pressure, breathing and electrical skin response when key words or thoughts are introduced into a conversation.

Although some people can learn to control even such involuntary processes as blood pressure, polygraphs have been used successfully not only by police officers but also by psychotherapists, who employ the instruments to detect deep-seated delusions or suppressed beliefs. The psychiatrist R. D. Laing described a schizophrenic patient who, while hooked up to a polygraph, was asked whether he was Napoleon. Hoping to be released from the hospital, the patient replied, "No, I am not" —and the apparatus immediately reported that he was telling a lie.

While many of these effects can be traced, indirectly at least, to the eminently useful fight-or-flight reaction *(Chapter 1)*, some, such as tears and laughter, cannot. They must be triggered by stress-caused nerve or hormone signals, but why they are triggered is unknown. One of the most common—and most puzzling—is laughter. The simultaneous contraction of 15 facial muscles, accompanied by loud, often irrepressible exhalations of breath, remains in large part a mystery. Physically, it may be related to the explosive sneeze or cough that expels an irritant from the respiratory tract—but that is hard to prove. Emotionally, it is more elusive. People laugh as cats purr and dogs wag their tails, in an expression of satisfaction, pleasure and friendship. But they laugh in other, less joyful ways as well—in ways clearly related to disturbing tension and stress. They laugh nervously when they are unsure of themselves, sarcastically as an expression of disbelief, even with a hint of savage delight when someone they do not like gets his comeuppance.

Attempts to explain laughter have occupied students of human behavior for millennia. A persistent idea holds that laughter, and its milder precursor smiling, is an expression of personal superiority. In ancient Greece, Aristotle suggested that a man's laughter was a reaction to the ugliness he perceived in others; 19 centuries later, the English philosopher Thomas Hobbes averred that "the passion of laughter is nothing else but sudden glory arising from a sudden conception of eminency in ourselves by comparison with the infirmity of others."

In 1860 the English social scientist Herbert Spencer suggested that laughter was a mechanism for the discharge of aggressive tension. He proposed that "nervous energy always tends to beget muscular motion," and that when "consciousness is unawares transferred from great things to small," the "liberated nerve force" expends itself along the channels of least resistance, the muscular movements of laughter. The same ideas of aggression and release were later reflected in Sigmund Freud's view of humor, which he saw as the momentary gratification of a forbidden wish, relieving anxiety and producing a sudden release of tension. More recently the author Arthur Koestler linked laughter with

Her face tense with fear, a girl walks past soldiers patrolling a street in strife-torn Northern Ireland. Although the girl is in no actual danger—the soldiers are protecting her, not threatening her—her body automatically reacts with fight-or-flight responses like those that protect the baboon under attack on page 121.

The nine-year-old guest of honor at an Italian birthday party undergoes a traditional custom—a sharp, even painful, tug on the ear for each year she has lived. Though the custom seems bizarre to most outsiders, this party prank is invariably greeted with gales of laughter in Italy.

The embarrassment of a man struggling into his pants after fleeing from a California hotel fire draws uncontrollable laughter from a woman who also fled the blaze. Even a helpful policeman cannot resist a chuckle at the man's predicament.

The mysteries
of laughter

To behavioral scientists, laughter is not funny. It is a serious matter, for it serves to relieve stress. But it is also something of a mystery, for its evolutionary purpose is a puzzle, and it is a normal reaction to many different and unrelated kinds of situations.

People laugh not only from pleasure or affection, but also at the discomfiture of someone else, as a means of releasing excess energy, as an expression of superiority or aggression, and even at the giving or receiving of pain *(left, above)*. But in all cases laughter performs the basic function of resolving emotional tension.

Laughter—aroused with the help of champagne and clowning at a banquet in Peking—helps German industrialists and their Chinese hosts shed the tensions generated by a series of nerve-racking negotiations on a trade agreement.

release: "The peculiar breathing in laughter, with its repeated, explosive exhalations, seems designed to puff away surplus tension in a kind of respiratory gymnastics; and the vigorous gestures and slapping of thighs obviously serve the same function."

Weeping seems the opposite of laughter. In place of laughter's expulsion of air in short, convulsive bursts, followed by long breath-catching intakes, the weeping body gasps for air in short, repeated intakes or sobs and expels it in long sighs or cries. Unlike laughter, weeping serves a clearly practical purpose: both tears and the flow of mucus associated with weeping wash away irritants from eyes and nose. But the evolution of weeping as an emotional response is as mysterious as that of laughter. One ingenious theory, proposed by Cornell University's Harold Wolff, suggests that weeping survives as a sort of conditioned reflex established in childhood. Infants cry and sob involuntarily in response to such elemental stresses as hunger, cold and fear —and the mechanism works; the infants' needs are met by concerned and apparently omnipotent parents. Later, Wolff said, an individual continues to employ this same physiological signal "to gain sympathy, support and protection for himself against many other threats from a hostile environment."

If weeping did evolve into a call for help, its role as a release for the tensions of sorrow seems a natural development. Weeping usually indicates distress rather than pleasure. Yet like laughter, it represents an all-purpose response from the body's limited repertoire to a broad range of situations. A beautiful painting or piece of music, a smile on the face of a child, the sweet sadness of some remembered love can bring a welling up of emotion, a breath-stopping, choking feeling and a misting of the eyes. So can feelings of deep gratitude, or sympathy when a friend, or even an actor on a stage, undergoes some personal ordeal. Relief, too, can bring tears as well as laughter, or a tug-of-war between the two.

In some cultures, this mechanism for release of stress has evolved into a form of social communication that can vary from an unconscious call for help to an expression of pure joy. It contributes not only to the relief of an individual but also to the solidarity of a tribe. Mourning rites in numerous societies require that the entire community gather for prolonged and elaborate wailing in honor of the deceased. Among such peoples as the Andaman Islanders and Australian aborigines, ceremonial crying conveys feelings not adequately expressed in any other way. The Andamese weep not only at marriages and initiation ceremonies—as people do at weddings and graduations in other parts of the world—but also on other joyful occasions. When two men who have been separated for some time meet again, they invariably celebrate the occasion by bursting into tears; and when two hostile groups finally settle their differences they hold a peace-making ceremony that is followed by a spell of communal weeping.

Even people who could not conceive of crying at every celebration, large or small, expect to weep in some situations. It is a normal reaction to stress, like laughter and goose flesh. There are also reactions that might be called abnormal, since the results are considered illnesses. They are not immediate responses, as normal ones are, but delayed, perhaps for years. They do not strike everyone, and if they do appear, their form varies from person to person.

Some abnormal reactions seem indirect; they come about because a normal reaction is prevented. The existence of the basic stress is denied, and its ordinary aftermath is suppressed—tears are held back, anxiety masked with a false smile, danger resolutely ignored—because the social situation seems to demand that course. Such conflicts between a discerned stress and the requirements of society have their own kind of survival value: society would soon fall apart if individuals gave in to every passing impulse to run away from their responsibilities, hold up a bank or bash their tormentors over the head. But the suppression of such conflicts, according to many authorities, can create a physical threat to the individual.

Other abnormal reactions to stress seem to be direct; they arise not because of any suppression of responses or denial of pressures but as a consequence of the stress itself. Such direct relationships between stress and illness have been blamed for a host of diseases, including even allergies, arthritis and cancer.

Scientific interest in the influence of the mind over physical health —psychosomatic medicine—reached a peak during the 1950s and 1960s. Masses of research data seemed to indicate that a great many human ills arose in the head, rather than from such prosaic agents as germs, bad diet or pollutants. Then the pendulum of opinion swung back; challenges were made to the psychosomatic explanations and descriptions of disease. These differences cannot be reconciled until more is learned about the complexly indirect effects of stress-initiated nerve and hormone signals. Meanwhile, the debate rages more fiercely than ever, and many physicians now take a cautious, middle-of-the-road view. Psychiatrist Richard Rahe, one of the inventors of the Holmes-Rahe scale *(page 91)*, spelled out this position: "Both physical and psychological factors make a contribution to illness," he wrote. "In some illnesses, such as botulism, the toxin [a physical factor] is so powerful that the physical factors scale is nearly at its extreme magnitude while the psychological factors scale is near zero. Conversely, in illnesses such as headache and low-back pain, the psychological factors scale approaches its highest magnitude and the physical factors scale drops to low levels." Most illnesses, in Rahe's opinion, fall between; coronary disease, for example, is caused almost equally by psychological and physical factors.

At one extreme of the spectrum suggested by Rahe are the peculiar ailments caused entirely by internal stress reactions, with no external physical basis whatever. They are the so-called conversion symptoms, or hysterias, in which the body develops clear-cut physical disorders —blindness, deafness or partial paralysis—as a response to some intolerable conflict. Sigmund Freud, whose early work was stimulated largely by the study of such symptoms, suggested that when a person cannot express an inner conflict directly, he may convert the conflict into a physical disability; the disability then relieves him of any need to face the situation that created the conflict in the first place. In short, an individual under stress may unconsciously try to solve his problem by getting sick, and he usually cannot see any relationship between his sickness and its actual cause until it is revealed to him through psychotherapy.

During World War II, psychiatrists applied Freud's theories to servicemen under stress, who frequently developed disabilities peculiarly related to their military duties. Among combat fliers the symptoms were almost wholly confined to the eyes and ears, the sensory organs vital to flying. After a series of missions over enemy territory, fliers often had blurring of vision, difficulties with depth perception, vertigo, headaches and deafness or pain in the ears. In a job in which precision formation flying and constant communication are a matter of life or death, such symptoms were of course sufficient to ground the fliers immediately. Among paratroopers, who must take the impact of landing before they can do anything else, the most frequent malady—and one particularly common on the eve of an especially dangerous mission—was weakness or paralysis in the legs. In peacetime situations, psychiatrists have observed that conversion symptoms often have more elusive but equally strong symbolic relationships with an emotional problem: a person who wishes he had never heard bad news may become deaf.

A conversion symptom has obvious value to the individual who suffers it: his sickness removes him from a situation he cannot handle and at the same time permits him to see himself not as a malingerer or one in-

In the stress-charged atmosphere of an air traffic control center, two men study a radar screen as they track a plane through congested skies. Their heavy responsibilities, one study indicates, may make them vulnerable to illness.

A tense job that causes disease

Although occupations involving high stress—such as politician, military commander, business executive—have long been suspect as dangers to health, proof linking stress to illness has been elusive. Some of the most convincing evidence is the distinctive afflictions of members of one of the most stressful professions: air traffic controllers.

The medical records of these specialists, who use radar, weather instruments and communications equipment to guide air transport, were analyzed by Sidney Cobb of the University of Michigan and Robert M. Rose of Boston University. They compared 5,199 controllers with 8,435 pilots who fly commercial cargo and hence are presumably subject to less stress. Factors such as genetics and diet were assumed to average out, and in order to eliminate the effects of age, the scientists did not compare illness occurrences directly. Instead, they used the pilots' records to calculate how many cases of each disease would be expected among the controllers if the two groups were identical. But the actual number of cases that appeared among the controllers *(orange bar)* was greater than the expected number *(gray bar)*.

THE AIR TRAFFIC CONTROLLERS' ILLNESSES

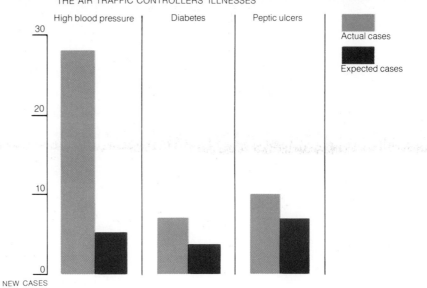

capable of solving his problems, but simply as a person who is sick. Many sufferers begin to relish their new role and the attention, affection and protection that they receive. And the retreat into a "sick role," some psychologists point out, can prove a convenient, though largely unconscious, solution not only for the patient but also for the people around him. A troubling or unacceptable mental state is transformed into a socially acceptable physical illness, and everyone can concentrate on getting the patient well. But when sickness becomes a habitual defense mechanism, a way of transforming recurrent psychological problems into treatable physical ones, still another psychosomatic disorder can appear: the person becomes a chronic hypochondriac.

Beyond the purely psychological illnesses classified as conversion symptoms lies the whole range of stress-related disease plotted by Richard Rahe—illnesses to which both stress and physical factors make their contributions in varying degrees. Exactly where in the scale they fall is a matter of continuing dispute. The evidence linking some of them to stress is tenuous, depending on subjective judgments of personality types or life styles—data always open to question—or based largely on the general observations of a few physicians.

Certain authorities have suggested that cancer, for example, is affected by stress. Dr. Eugene P. Pendergrass, a past president of the American Cancer Society, noted that many of his own patients seemed to be living comfortably after successful treatment only to have the death of a son or the burden of long unemployment reactivate the disease, with fatal results. A more detailed analysis of 450 cancer patients over a dozen years was made by Lawrence LeShan of New York's Institute of Applied Biology. He reported that the most typical cases had at some point in early life suffered a severe emotional trauma, such as the loss of a parent. After that experience they apparently came to feel that emotional relationships could bring desertion and pain. As a result, they shied away from all but superficial ties until they finally found another channel for their emotional energies—the role of a parent, or a particularly satisfying job. Then this channel was blocked: they were fired from the job or their children grew up and no longer needed them. Though some made desperate efforts to find yet another attachment, the stress of loss returned in force, and the zest went out of living. In some cases, the first symptoms of cancer appeared as early as six months after their crucial loss.

The data implicating stress in cancer is too limited to give anyone cause for concern—or grounds for hope—about the relationship. This disease is near the low end of Richard Rahe's comparison, at the opposite extreme from the totally stress-caused conversion symptoms. Several other diseases fall closer to the middle. There are many observations connecting them to stress, but no clear consensus among the experts about a cause-and-effect relationship. Among these ailments are two—arthritis and allergy—that are intricately involved with one of the body's vital defense mechanisms, the immune system, which mobilizes internal processes to fight off invasion by alien substances such as germs, viruses and poisons.

The evidence linking arthritis to stress is largely circumstantial. Doctors have long known that flare-ups of rheumatoid arthritis often accompany emotional crises or problems, and that victims tend to have certain personality traits in common: many are dominating persons who use hard physical exertion as an outlet for aggressive feelings. Close to three quarters of these victims are women, and they tend to run to a single psychological subtype: tireless housewives and selfless mothers, who keep their husbands and children under firm control. As these women grow older the outlets of hard work and exercise become more difficult, and enforced inactivity apparently sets the stage for trouble. Exactly what brings on the arthritis is not certain, but some specialists believe it may be a combination of emotional stress, muscle tension and biochemical changes within the body. According to one theory, these changes arise from the immune system, which sets off an inappropriate defense reaction by the body to its own tissues.

Inappropriate and damaging defense reactions—essentially, failures of the immune systems—are the basis of allergy. Millions of people are allergic, or easily irritated, by a bewildering variety of specific materials, including dust, pollen, cat or dog hair, eggs, shellfish and pork. When an allergic person comes in contact with his special enemy, his extreme defense reactions release in his body such chemicals as histamine, which helps to cause swelling of the mucous membranes in the nose and itching in the eyes. Many allergists agree that stress—overwork, anxiety or resentment—can precipitate attacks or make them worse. Certainly, psychological stimuli are significant in these ailments: people suffering from allergies often become hypersensitive to the very idea of their nemesis, and researchers have induced allergic attacks in the absence of the irritating agent by showing pollen-sensitive subjects pictures of fields in bloom, or people allergic to horses a photograph of a horse, or subjects sensitive to goldfish an empty goldfish bowl.

The most common serious allergic disease is asthma, which according to a United Nations survey afflicts as much as 5 per cent of the populations of developed countries. Here, too, stress is a significant factor. Young asthmatics are more prone to attacks when they are emotionally excited. Often, the emotions that bring on asthma are related to the child's relation with his mother. Alarmed by the first attack, she becomes overprotective. Such measures may be well-intentioned and even advisable, but they can backfire. Out of resentment at the curbs upon his freedom, the child may start to react not to ragweed or a similar irritant, but to his mother, wheezing and choking when the irritant is nowhere about, as if to shut out and wash away an offensive thought.

While the case against stress in arthritis and allergies may not be airtight, far more significant data is available about other ailments. Three classes of disease in particular—headaches and backaches, stomach and duodenal ulcers, and high blood pressure—lie near the high end of Richard Rahe's comparison; stress is clearly a cause, if not the cause.

Bodily pain can come from muscles that are kept contracted over prolonged periods, and muscular contraction is a normal reaction to stress. As many as nine out of 10 headaches, some specialists estimate, arise in prolonged contraction of the muscles of the neck and head, a readiness to spring into a physical action that never takes place. Such tension headaches can begin in long hours of alertness while driving in heavy traffic or studying for a tough examination; they can begin, too, in a minor but persistent problem at home or on the job. In all of these situations some people seem to brace themselves to carry an unwelcome load, tightening the muscles of their shoulders as well as their neck and jaws. If these muscles stay contracted for long periods without release, they too may produce pain, sending it up the back of the head, down the neck and over the shoulder blades, to the lower back and even the legs and arms—indeed, to almost any part of the body where muscles can be held constantly and unconsciously taut. If the tension persists, the muscles readily acquire the habit of overreacting. The result of such overwork may be excruciating chronic pain. The Civil War diary of Ulysses S. Grant reveals how headaches can be triggered by stress and cured when stress is removed. When Grant's opponent, Robert E. Lee, refused to surrender on the eve of Appomattox, Grant experienced such a severe headache that he had to take to his bed. Then, when a messenger brought word that Lee had changed his mind, Grant noted with wonderment that the pain in his head disappeared almost instantly.

Even more than headaches, ulcers are commonly linked with stress, and properly so. Two types, stomach and duodenal ulcers, in which digestive acids eat away the linings of the stomach and small intestine, seem to afflict stress-prone personalities. They generally strike individ-

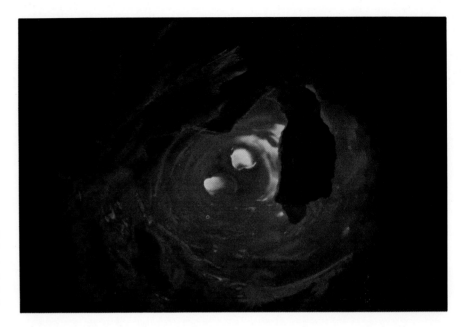

Like a stalactite in an eerily lit cavern, a blood clot partially blocks an artery narrowed by cholesterol-corrugated walls. Stress can release cholesterol and also, by contracting a partly blocked artery, can stop blood flow and cause death.

uals whose need to be loved conflicts with an urge to dominate and excel; an ulcer attack is frequently triggered by a serious loss, such as the death of a spouse or discharge from a job.

Many researchers associate ulcers with a life style rife with frustrations. And when stress patterns change, so does the incidence of ulcers. Under the domestic rigors and repressions of the Victorian Age, ulcers were not a man's but a woman's disease; seven women got ulcers to every three men. As life became easier on women (or harder on men) the ratio changed dramatically: by the 1950s some nine out of 10 ulcer sufferers were male. Today, however, as more and more women enter the competition of business, professional and political life, the incidence of stomach problems among them is creeping up again.

Just as much a stereotype of a stress disease as ulcers are afflictions that ordinary people lump under the term heart trouble—any ailment of the cardiovascular system. In the world's industrialized and urbanized nations—those where stress is supposedly severe—such illnesses have become the leading cause of death, primarily among the old and male, but increasingly among the young and female as well. Whether there is a generalized cause-and-effect relationship is a matter of dispute —among the most controversial studies are those of Meyer Friedman and Ray Rosenman of San Francisco's Mount Zion Hospital and Medical Center, who maintain there are distinctive "Type A" and "Type B" personalities indicating susceptibility to heart disease. But there is no dispute that at least one cardiovascular illness—high blood pressure, which afflicts one in every six Americans—does involve stress.

Blood-pressure changes are one of the normal, inevitable reactions to stress. To many threats, real or imagined, the body responds instantly to autonomic-nerve signals by constricting the muscles of the arterial walls. Blood pressure rises, and an emergency oversupply of blood rushes through the body while the other mechanisms of the alarm reaction come into play *(page 16)*. When the reaction passes, the blood pressure ordinarily drops—but not if the alarm state continues in the form of subconscious fear, hostility or anxiety. Then, pressure remains high, and both the arteries and the complex network of smaller blood vessels are subjected to prolonged, possibly damaging, strain. Even when the brain finally calls the emergency off, the pressure may drop by a smaller amount each time, eventually stabilizing at a permanently high level.

Stress may also contribute to chronic high blood pressure in still another way. One factor in this ailment appears to be the levels of certain substances in the blood, particularly one called cholesterol. Cholesterol is believed to cause the arteries to harden and clog, so that greater pressure is called for to force blood through the narrowed, inelastic passages. Cholesterol build-up is blamed largely on a rich diet. Largely, but not entirely, for a rise in cholesterol level can also be caused by stress, particularly the stress of frustration and emotional conflict.

The fact has been proved in many experiments, including some inspired by a certain perverse ingenuity. At the National Institutes of Health cholesterol levels were compared in blood samples taken about five minutes apart. The first sample was taken from a relaxed, comfortably resting patient by a friendly, informal doctor, who seemed to regard the test as routine and inconsequential. Then a second doctor entered the room. His attitude was serious and foreboding; he wore surgical gown and mask and carried a large hypodermic needle. Explaining that he was about to apply "adrenal stimulation," he turned the patient on his side, swabbed and chilled his lower back with alcohol, and announced: "This local anesthetic will prevent *most* of the pain. There is no danger if you hold perfectly still." After five minutes of such ominous preparation, this second doctor took a blood sample. Its cholesterol level had soared above that of the first sample, and the level was still rising in samples taken 10 minutes later.

As part of another experiment, Dr. Stewart Wolf of the University of Texas altered levels of blood cholesterol, technically "serum cholesterol," simply by switching conversations to stressful subjects. His procedure is best described in his own words: "When we simply talked to the patients for an hour about ships and shoes and sealing wax and tried to be encouraging and friendly, the serum cholesterol usually fell.

continued on page 138

A volcanic struggler

The Type A may "bristle with the barely governable rage that seethes so often just below the surface." Among the signs of inner turmoil: clenched or table-pounding fists, nervous tics and grinding teeth.

Osborn

The tempestuous Type A

For some people, stress is chronic, palpable and incessant—the mainstay of their personalities. Two cardiologists, Meyer Friedman and Ray Rosenman, believe that such an aggressive hard-driving personality, which they label Type A, is headed for trouble. Their studies suggest that the stressful Type A pattern of behavior is an independent—and possibly the most significant —factor in causing heart attacks.

In books and lectures, the two heart specialists have warned the public about the dangers of being a Type A. Excerpts from their writings characterize the ill-fated Type A in the captions for caricatures *(above and overleaf)* by cartoonist Robert Osborne.

A chronic hurrier

"The most significant trait of the Type A man is his habitual sense of time urgency." He *"incessantly strives to accomplish too much,"* noted Friedman and Rosenman, *"in the amount of time he allots for these purposes."*

A combative challenger

Aggression comes out in Type A men in their "tendency always to compete with or to challenge other people, whether the activity consists of a sporting contest, a game of cards or a simple discussion."

An exasperated dawdler

A Type A finds it "anguishing to wait in a line or to wait . . . to be seated at a restaurant." Lengthy books, repetitious chores and situations that result in inefficiency are also anathemas.

One-man band

"Striving to think of or do two or more things simultaneously . . . is one of the commonest traits in a Type A man"—a characteristic that Friedman and Rosenman term polyphasic.

In stressful interviews, on the other hand, dealing with topics of significant personal conflict, serum cholesterol usually rose and sometimes there was a very substantial increase, as much as 40 per cent."

Those serious effects of stress on the circulatory system are accepted by nearly all medical scientists. They acknowledge that stress can cause chronic high blood pressure and, temporarily at least, an increase in cholesterol levels. But there is no such consensus about direct effects of stress on the heart itself. Most authorities believe that stress may cause a heart failure in someone who already has a diseased heart, but they are skeptical that stress causes the disease in the first place. They blame heart ailments on diet and smoking, and cite mountains of statistics to prove their points. This doubt about the relationship between heart disease and stress runs counter to the common notion that the fast-paced, hard-driving business executive is doomed to sudden death from a heart attack. There is evidence on both sides of the argument.

Perhaps the most widely publicized indictment of stress in heart attacks is that of Friedman and Rosenman. Although some attempts to duplicate their research have produced different results, the influence of their concepts has been widely felt; when a popular statement of their views, *Type A Behavior and Your Heart,* was published in paperback, more than 500,000 copies were printed.

After more than 30 years studying coronary disease in the hospital, the laboratory and their consultation rooms, Friedman and Rosenman concluded that at least half the people who get heart attacks could be definitively linked to none of the known or suspected causes such as smoking, diet, exercise habits and contributing disease. Some of these causes, they argued, account for only a minority of cases. In discussing the mysterious factor of "maleness"—about two thirds of all heart-attack victims in the United States are men—Friedman points out: "Although American women seem to be protected from heart trouble, Mexican women have as much heart disease as their men. It is also one to one in Southern Italy, but it is four to one in Northern Italy."

What, then, is the missing explanation of susceptibility to heart disease? According to Friedman and Rosenman, the answer lies in a distinctive pattern of personality and behavior, marked by excessive competitive drive, aggressiveness, impatience and a harrying sense of urgency and time. Friedman and Rosenman consider this Type A pattern to be a characteristic not of middle-class business executives alone, but one that is common among urban dwellers of virtually every occupation and class, from florists to policemen, and increasingly so among younger people and women as well as men.

Type A's, who in varying degrees of intensity make up close to 60 per cent of the people the two doctors have studied, resemble people almost everyone knows. They generally strive to accomplish too much or participate in too many activities, trying to stuff more and more into less and less time. In their attempts to save time they create deadlines if none exist, become obsessed with numbers and quantities rather than quality as a measure of success. Many have an aggressive drive that borders on habitual hostility. They generally have few hobbies or diversions outside their work, and feel vaguely guilty when they relax. Significantly, they also abuse their own bodies. Type A's tend to eat rich foods, smoke and drink more than the average; and except for an occasional, hard-fought game of golf or tennis, they consider regular physical exercise boring and a waste of time. In 1974, the doctors announced their findings in the largest and most elaborate of their studies, a continued monitoring of 3,500 Californians over a period of 10 years. The figures showed that the Type A men, on the average, were almost three times more likely than the Type B's to get coronary heart disease.

In many ways, the results were oddly reminiscent of one of the classic studies in psychosomatic medicine, a survey of 1,600 hospital patients reported over 30 years earlier, in 1943, by Dr. Flanders Dunbar, at New York City's Columbia Presbyterian Medical Center. In her pioneer work, Dunbar attempted to match up personality traits and emotional problems with disorders of various kinds. Among the heart-attack patients, she observed, were many highly trained professionals and self-made men who seemed to have difficulty sharing their responsibilities and getting along with others. The more trying life became, the unhappier these patients were, and the unhappier they became, the harder they worked. Dunbar described their most salient characteristic as "compulsive striving." As she put it, "They would rather die than fail."

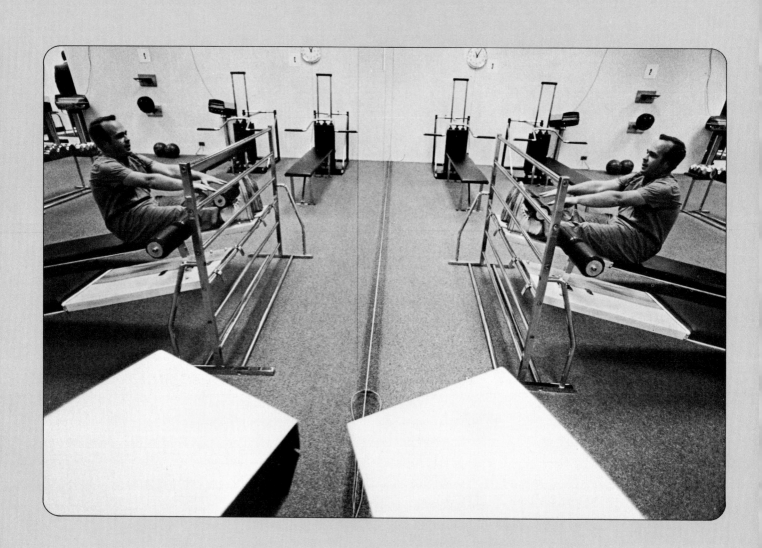

Working Off Steam

5

In bustling, noisy Rio de Janeiro, a suicide-prevention service named Telepeace handles an average of 1,000 calls a day from anxious individuals, counseling them on their problems and referring them to places where they can go for help. In the quiet green Bavarian countryside, an ultramodern clinic puts overstressed girls through a six-week program of physical conditioning, career guidance and general recreation so they can go back home and cope more effectively with their lives. In Bangkok, thousands tune in regularly to television and radio programs on the problems of everyday living conducted by Thailand's leading psychiatrist and director of mental health, whose two books on the subject have sold over a million copies. In London, Manila and San Francisco, executives, salesmen, secretaries and housewives flock to physical fitness classes, yoga sessions, meditation lectures and psychotherapy groups. And almost everywhere, countless men and women suffering from undefined worries and tensions reach for more familiar home remedies: a martini or a glass of wine, a cigarette, a soothing piece of apple strudel or chocolate cake—and pills, pills, pills.

All these far-flung efforts to counter the tensions of life support a flourishing stress industry. West Germans spent more than six billion dollars on vacations abroad in a single year, while Americans spent over five billion dollars and Canadians nearly two billion dollars. Organized, all-inclusive eight- or 14-day "antistress" programs are among the attractions that bring more than 100,000 visitors a year to the famous German spa of Baden-Baden. The Japanese spent more than three billion dollars in 1973 on various sports facilities, including golf courses for some 8.5 million players. More alcohol than gasoline is concocted in the world; most of this ocean of relaxing liquid is unmeasured, but the legally reported quantities suggest the amounts: per capita consumption in Sweden and the United Kingdom is eight quarts a year, in France 24, in Italy 16, in the United States 11.

The modern drugs that specifically counteract stress—the tranquilizers—are the most common of all remedies prescribed by physicians. More than a quarter of a billion dollars' worth of one brand alone was sold in the United States in one year. Such pills are taken by nearly one person in every five in France and Belgium, and by nearly as large a proportion of the populations of other Western countries: 16 per cent in Sweden, 15 per cent in Denmark and the United States, 14 per cent in Germany and the United Kingdom, 13 per cent in the Netherlands, 11 per cent in Italy and 10 per cent in Spain.

Some popular stress relievers are loaded with potential danger for their users. In the more affluent nations millions of extra pounds of fat —accompanied by increased risks of heart disease and other disorders —are carried around by men, women and children who have learned that when they are feeling a little lonely or depressed the rewards of a sweet or a gourmet dinner can temporarily assuage the pain. Alcoholism itself is a major health problem in the Soviet Union, Scandinavia, Ireland and the United States, as well as a chief cause of traffic accidents, liver disease and divorce. The soothing effects of smoking, too, are often purchased at a tragic long-term price. Cigarettes have been indicted not only in lung cancer, chronic bronchitis and emphysema but also in heart disease; there is some research indicating that the nicotine in the smoke stimulates the nervous system to release the stress hormon norepinephrine, which pushes up blood pressure and releases fatty substances like cholesterol.

There are, however, new techniques aimed at relieving stress effects by enabling the individual to control his physical reactions or achieve a more philosophical, healthier attitude toward the pressures and urgencies of everyday life. They seem to counteract directly the internal physiological responses of stress. And beyond these new methods lie a host of traditional approaches that long have enabled people to gain a greater measure of control over the tempo of their lives and reduce the disabling effects of stressful living. Some of these methods involve such simple expedients as diet changes or programs of regular exercise. Others call for a reordering of daily priorities, deliberate slowing down of the pace of life or even a complete change of life styles.

The initiative for these programs must, of course, come from the individual himself, but cultures and institutions can be helpful to the stress sufferer. Socially accepted mourning rituals, such as funerals and wakes, can ease the burden of the extreme stress accompanying the death of a family member. Formal religions provide helpful perspectives and comfort in troubling times. And for some, the deliberate exposure to physical hardships and dangers in organized stress-seeking groups toughens resistance and frequently reveals totally unsuspected sources of strength.

Among the new approaches to stress control, one of the most unusual is the technique known as biofeedback, or visceral learning, in which signals such as clicking tones or flashing lights help teach people to control their own irregular heartbeats, high blood pressure, chronic headaches or hyperactive stomachs. The method involves giving a reward for progress toward an indicated goal—a technique long used by circus-animal trainers and more recently by scientists in experiments that teach pigeons to play games and chimpanzees to converse in sign language. In this case the reward is a psychological one—the flashing light or clicking tone—and the goal is the application of a faculty that most people are unaware they possess: mental control over the autonomic nervous system. Since this system is the principal one involved in stress *(Chapter 2)*, control over it, in theory, should enable an individual to manage his stresses at will.

In one demonstration of visceral learning, five patients with the irregular heartbeat called arrythmia were trained to restore normal rhythms. Each patient, lying on a hospital bed, was connected to an instrument that measured his heartbeat while he watched three colored lights—a green one that glowed when the rate was too slow, a red for a fast beat and a yellow for normal. He was asked to try to keep the yellow light on by willing his heart to speed up or slow down. These subjects succeeded not so much by thinking about their hearts as by concentrating on something else—one increased his heart rate by thinking about bouncing a ball, another by mentally running down a dark street, and still another slowed his heart by lying still and staring at the lights. Since these early experiments, the use of biofeedback has spread widely and proponents claim that thousands of patients have been helped. Some have learned how to fend off painful tension headaches by relaxing the muscles in their foreheads, others to avoid piercing migraines by "thinking" their hands warm and thus, through some mysterious response in the circulatory system, preventing the direct cause of migraine, the expansion of blood vessels in the scalp.

The ability to control supposedly uncontrollable bodily reactions —particularly those now known to be stress responses—has long been claimed by mystics of the Orient. For centuries practitioners of yoga, Sufi and Zen have used individual meditation, sometimes accompanied by rigorous physical training, austere diets and gymnastic body postures, to achieve heightened states of consciousness and well-being, as

well as extraordinary control over breathing, heartbeat and other bodily processes long thought to be beyond the influence of the conscious mind. Twentieth Century investigations of these claims have shown that they are not fakes. A team of American and Indian researchers—M. A. Wenger of the University of California at Los Angeles, B. K. Bagchi of the University of Michigan and B. K. Anand of the All-India Institute of Medical Sciences—found that some yogis could slow heartbeat and normal breathing rates. In Japan, Y. Sugi and K. Akutsu discovered that Zen monks were able to reduce their consumption of oxygen and production of carbon dioxide—evidence that their bodies' output of energy had declined, the opposite of the effect produced by stress.

Westerners' quest for stress relief (and new experiences) has led many to take up various forms of Eastern mysticism. The most popular is transcendental meditation, a practice introduced to the West in the early 1960s by an Indian monk named Maharishi Mahesh Yogi. By the mid-1970s "TM" could claim over a million devotees around the world, roughly half of them in the United States, with another 15,000 or more being added to the ranks every month; among its better-known converts are American football superstar Joe Namath and stress expert Hans Selye himself.

Part of the appeal of TM—whose promoters have a grand plan of training enough teachers to instruct everyone in the world—is its almost incredible simplicity; after two evening lectures, an hour of individual training and a quaint initiation ceremony (involving a white handkerchief, some fresh flowers and two pieces of fresh fruit), the new meditator receives his "mantra." This is a short, easily pronounced but meaningless sound like "karom," which he can repeat to himself, eyes closed and body relaxed, to achieve a state of conscious restfulness for 20 minutes twice a day, at home, in the office or even on the way to work. The meditator takes one minute to relax himself before going into meditation, and two minutes to "reactivate" himself, or bring himself out of it. During the 20-minute period, he simply lets his mind wander free, thinking about whatever might occur to him. He does not have to think about anything in particular, not even his mantra, but the fact that he has been given a mantra for meditative purposes causes it to come to mind frequently. "I play games with my mantra; I make anagrams with it," says one practitioner.

The surprising thing about such meditation is not only its simplicity but also the fact that it seems to work for numbers of people. Studies by two Harvard doctors, physiologist Robert Keith Wallace and cardiologist Herbert Benson, indicate that regular meditation can counteract stress. Wallace and Benson tested 28 men and eight women who had been trained in the techniques of transcendental meditation. The experiments showed that when the subjects meditated, their bodies relaxed in such a way as to reverse the reactions associated with stress. A reduction in the consumption of oxygen and the release of carbon dioxide indicated that the rate of energy production, which increases with stress, had gone down. Blood pressure, another direct indicator of stress, was not reduced by meditation itself; pressure went down during the relaxation preceding meditation, but it then stayed at the low level. Still another indicator of stress—the skin's resistance to electricity—declined. And the concentration of a chemical called lactate, which is known to increase when stress occurs, also decreased sharply.

Wallace and Benson believe that these effects differ markedly from the relaxation accompanying normal sleep or hypnosis. Sleep causes opposite changes in such responses as skin resistance and energy production, and hypnosis causes only the changes suggested by the hyp-

notist. Although visceral learning can yield many of the results achieved by meditation, biofeedback seems to work more specifically. Meditation is an antistress remedy, Wallace and Benson suggest: "It looks very much like a counterpart of the fight-or-flight reaction," and, they conclude, "may indicate a guidepost to better health."

The benefits of such specialized stress-relieving techniques as deep meditation and biofeedback training are restricted to relatively few people. Similar limitations circumscribe the influence of the "encounter" groups, which bring people together to share normally censored emotions in a release of feeling, and of stress-training programs like Outward Bound *(pages 160-171)*, which seek to toughen people to resist everyday strains by exposing them to physical hardship. But there are many avenues of stress relief open to nearly anyone. No scientific instruments, special training or organized groups are needed to eat a sensible diet, take regular exercise, make constructive use of leisure and slow down a frenetic life style.

Perhaps the most basic of all stress-relief measures in sedentary, luxury-prone societies is one that doctors are forever advocating to their patients: a certain amount of regular, honest physical exercise, along with a diet that does not lean heavily on sugars, starches and fats. As one of England's leading stress researchers, Malcolm Carruthers, pointed out, most adults could cut their food intake almost in half without endangering their health, particularly if they avoided sugary, starchy confections. Moreover, Carruthers noted, high stress levels—measured in cholesterol concentrations, high blood pressure and blood clotting rate—decrease markedly when a person exercises regularly.

In experiments with hundreds of subjects at the London City Gymnasium, Carruthers found that as little as 15 minutes of varied and properly designed exercises two or three times a week enabled most of the subjects to do three to six times as much work for a given pulse rate, to reduce sharply their levels of cholesterol and to act less fatigued and more even-tempered most of the time. Carruthers, like many other doctors, is a strong proponent of doing exercises, rather than viewing them; tests of spectators at football games, he observes, have shown that their pulse rates often increase 40 per cent, and that the extra fats and sugars released into their bloodstreams are not dissipated by physical exertion, as they are by the players on the field.

Violent games like football, Carruthers adds, are not the answer for flabby middle-aged types; he leans toward swimming, bicycling and gymnasium exercises. Carruthers has undoubtedly enraged some of his countrymen (and delighted others) by his acerb assessment of one international form of exercise, golf. He considers it mostly a fine way to spoil a good walk, accompanied as it often is by such stress-makers as fierce competition, business conferences, frustratingly slow players, annoyingly lost balls, ineffective swings and the generally infuriating nature of the game itself.

Although the physical effort of exercise has always provided relief from stress, it has only recently been undertaken for that purpose. Daily work was once largely physical, and respite from muscular labor was sought in free time. Now that exercise is no longer so necessary for earning a living, it joins the many other activities—amusements, hobbies, vacations, travel—that are pursued for their own value, as safety valves to let off the pressures of everyday life. The need for outside interests is great for everyone, no matter what his daily tasks. The mother preoccupied with housekeeping and the assembly line worker tightening screws every day seek diversion from the stress of monotonous tasks; the executive who jets from country to country finds relaxation in doing things with his hands.

An ongoing private life balances work, providing different concerns, different values and the different ties and friendships that can accrue as a result. Winston Churchill became a dedicated and enthusiastic painter after he was 40 years old. Less famous but no less happy with their avocations are the bank president who prints books on a hand press; the corporation head who took up the oboe at the age of 40 and now plays regularly in the symphony orchestra near his home; the chairman of a chemical firm who became an authority on hummingbirds. And uncounted ordinary folk have found pleasure and release in everything from reading, fishing, gardening and stamp-collecting to kiteflying.

If people find in hobbies an antidote for daily pressures and a sense of accomplishment not always available on the job, they look to vacations as special opportunities for change and diversion. Most unwind on holidays by finding something new to see, sports to participate in or simply unstructured days someplace away from home. But especially in Europe, a unique type of vacation is meant to aid health and particularly to relieve stress. This is the promise of the spa, a resort built near springs of mineral-rich and supposedly beneficial warm water.

The most famous of spas is Baden-Baden, in Germany near the French border. The Roman Emperor Caracalla took its baths in the Third Century, although how much good they did him is disputed. Modern visitors come to cure all sorts of ailments, but stress is a common reason for what amounts to a comfortable vacation with a great many baths. An American physician who visited Baden-Baden, Karl Neumann, signed up for a two-hour treatment consisting of 19 baths, including two at 150° and one of ice water. In one bathhouse, he reported, "There are entire floors filled with bathtubs of all shapes and sizes possessing more valves and pipes than a ship's boiler. You can have half-baths, ascending baths, partial baths, alternating baths and showers, electric tub baths and even underwater massages. If you prefer—or your doctor prescribes—you can have water sprayed at you at any reasonable pressure, directly or by underwater jet. Your bath water can be 'spiked' with mud, oxygen, air bubbles and carbon dioxide." Such treatments are frequently prescribed by European physicians—139 scientific papers on the subject were published in 1972 and 1973. But American authorities are skeptical of the true therapeutic value, Neumann noted, believing that "if you remove a person from the everyday stresses of home and work, let him relax and spend time in warm water, that person will certainly feel better—whether the underlying pathological process is altered or not."

Making people feel better is, of course, the major purpose of vacations. Unfortunately they do not always achieve that goal. Vacations can become not a release from stress, but a major source of it. The summer vacation in particular, a cherished tradition, often produces as many problems as it solves. Many psychiatrists and marriage counselors report that their business peaks during the first week in September, when the holidays end and some families drag themselves home not refreshed but let-down, irritable and at each other's throats.

Most unhappy vacations, the counselors find, stem from unrealistic expectations; husbands may be looking for one thing, wives another, children something else, and they often fail to analyze their individual desires or make them clear to each other before they set off on the holiday. When people are crammed into a hot automobile or are competing for a crowded campsite, observed California psychologist George Bach, latent hostilities reach a flash point in a surprisingly short time. One woman, he recalled, became so furious over her husband's timidity in dealing with the room clerk at their hotel that she exploded with rage in the kitchenette of the suite to which they were finally assigned. She yelled, "I could kill you!" Just as furious, he handed her a bread knife and dared her to go ahead. She did.

The point to be remembered about vacations, Bach emphasized, is that they do not bring any automatic relaxing of tensions and stress. "Anything joyful has to be planned," he wrote. Most families can stay together for only about 72 hours without a break, Bach found, and he ad-

A group of Russian men banish stress in the warm spring water of a public bath at Tskhaltube in Soviet Georgia. Opportunities for "taking the waters" range from such baths (Moscow alone has 72) to the full-scale spa at Baden-Baden boasting mineralized, slightly radioactive water and an antistress program of lectures, concerts and organized games. The therapy works, for diversion, congenial company and warm water to relax muscles all help to dissipate stress.

vised frequent breaks to do something alone. If what a woman really needs is a vacation from mothering and housework, Bach observed, it is hardly a vacation for her if the children troop along and she has to cook; a real change for her would be a few days in a luxury resort with her husband, being waited on by others. If a man really wants to use his vacation to get to know his wife or children better, Bach added, he should not try to handle them all at once but plan to spend some time with each one in turn, sharing a day of fishing or hiking or loafing or whatever each enjoys most.

The difficulty some people have in unwinding on holiday stems from deep emotional conflicts. The holiday, like aspirin for arthritis, may temporarily stop superficial symptoms but does not alleviate the basic cause. A man who hates his job might manage to forget it while away for a few weeks, but when he returns, the work will seem more unpleasant than ever; in his case the vacation simply intensifies his workaday stress. What he needs is not a vacation but a different job, difficult as that may be to arrange.

Job boredom and alienation—as measured by absenteeism—are estimated to cost industry as much as $50 billion a year in the United States alone. Not surprisingly, however, the dissatisfaction is greatest among those who can least afford to do anything drastic about it. Three independent surveys of job holders in 16 different industries and areas near them demonstrated this fact. They show that 90 per cent or more of people in relatively independent, high-status positions—university professors, physicians, lawyers—would choose similar work if they had the option, while as few as 16 per cent of unskilled workers on automobile assembly lines would pick the same jobs again if they had the choice. Though job satisfaction studies indicate that money is a factor, they indicate a heavier emphasis on feelings of autonomy, responsibility, participation in planning, recognition from co-workers and the boss, and a sense of personal pride in the work done.

There is another type of person who is unable to find long-range lessening of stress in vacations. He does not hate his work; quite the opposite. He is so committed to the job he feels lost and depressed away from it. "He cannot rely on his inner resources," wrote Alexander Reid Martin, the analyst who extensively studied this fear of leisure. "He becomes a 'spoil sport' for himself and others." As a patient of Martin's described it: "I anticipate vacations. I think of the good time. Then, when the weekend comes, I waste my weekend. I waste my vacations."

When the stress is too great to be relieved by ordinary means such as recreation and holidays, it ought to be removed. Few people manage to do so, for a drastic change in life style is generally required. One who did is Meyer Friedman, co-father of the Type A theory. Friedman was neither wrapped up in nor repelled by his work. But he went at both work and play with the same intense drive. He was a prototype of the Type A personality he defined. Then he suffered a heart attack. He began studiously following a Type B pattern, even to wearing tweedy old sports jackets that helped him play the part. He moved out of the city to a placid nearby suburb, gave up cocktail parties, his pipe, membership on all committees except one, and read books he could not possibly rush through.

Friedman is a firm believer in purposely allotting more time to various activities than they might appear to require. Instead of getting up in the morning barely in time to grab some breakfast and rush off to work, he advised his patients to arise 15 to 20 minutes earlier; the time can be well spent on almost anything—doing a few exercises, reading the newspaper, or even taking a stroll in the yard without having to look nervously at a watch every minute.

Once at the office, Friedman recommended cutting down on all but the most important phone calls and sorting messages into different piles: those requiring prompt replies, permissible delays and no response at all. He suggested frequent breaks during the day for daydreaming or looking out the window, and at lunch hour, he advocated skipping a heavy meal in favor of wandering around the city—walking in the park one day, visiting a museum or browsing in a bookstore the next, going into a church, or just watching other people pass by. Along about mid-afternoon at work, he said, too many people pressure themselves to finish all their chores by 5 o'clock—just in time to battle the height of the rush hour in a frantic attempt to get home quickly.

In place of this doubly stressful routine, Friedman suggested slowing down a little and staying a half hour or so later when necessary, avoiding both the tensions of the last-minute office scramble and the frustrations of traffic. Among his other secret weapons against "hurry sickness," he recommended such simple devices as listening quietly as other people talk, not trying to think of more than one thing at a time, and carrying around a book to read in odd moments.

Like many students of stress, Friedman believed that people are at their self-destructive worst when driving a car; short of walking, bicycling or taking public transportation, his rather whimsical advice to people who drive is that they purposely not pass a slower car even if the chance arises. Whenever a person catches himself speeding up to get through a yellow light, Friedman proposed that he penalize himself by

continued on page 157

Dressed in coarse-woven ceremonial mourning clothes, relatives of a Chinese man kneel at his graveside in Taiwan. The mourners hold symbolic red lanterns to guide the dead man to a place where he will join his ancestors and become a kindly spirit watching over the welfare of the family. In this Taoist ritual, much of the stress of mourning is eased by such symbols, which help to assure the bereaved that the spirit of the dead remains part of their family.

Easing the pain of grief

All over the world, the great stress of a death is acknowledged—and assuaged—by prescribed ceremonies. Many are almost universal—the symbols of Taiwan *(above)*, the ritual wailing of the Pacific Islands and the feasting of Indonesia, Africa and Mexico *(overleaf)* have counterparts elsewhere.

Such ceremonies are essential in relieving stress, behavioral scientists believe, and much present-day suffering is blamed on neglect of old rituals in modern cultures. "A funeral rite," noted anthropologist Raymond Firth,

"benefits not the dead but the living." It reassures survivors by demonstrating family cohesion. Neighbors and friends share the grief, encouraging its release, assuming part of its burden and also providing distraction to lead away from self-pity. Even the drinking, dancing and feasting of some rites affect the body in ways that ease tension.

Perhaps most important, mourning observances strengthen belief in the hereafter, assuring those left behind that a loved one is not lost altogether but exists in spirit beyond death.

A community of Dani in West Irian wails
together for a tribeswoman in communal
crying that spreads grief, lessening its
impact. The weeping ritual is preceded
by a feast—and the food itself may serve
a purpose in easing stress. According to a
controversial study by anthropologist
Roy Rappaport, such nourishment
helps the body to respond to stress.

Exquisite offerings of fruit and flowers
mark cremation rites ending the 10-month
mourning astrologers decreed for a
Balinese king. Such a defined mourning
regulates grief. It sets a time to adjust
to death, gives release from inappropriate
activities, and schedules a return to
everyday life—with, in this case, a
celebration of the king's ascent to heaven.

Brightly garbed Banileke men dance
and sing in African rites at the conclusion
of a year's mourning for a dead comrade.
The dancers belong to the same secret
society as the deceased man did; through
their ceremonial dancing they not only
publicly display and work out their own
feelings of grief, but they also share
its impact with his mourning family.

At a South Korean funeral, food and
drink ease stress as relatives—wearing
traditional white—and friends partake of
a feast that includes much rice wine.
Alcohol, the oldest and commonest
tranquilizer, is often prescribed for grief,
but the manner of its use here—in a social
setting as part of a ritual—is believed
to enhance its value in relieving stress.

In Mexico, the Day of the Dead brings candle-bearing mourners to a cemetery. This important religious festival, on November 1, reinforces spiritual ties between living and dead, affirming continuity of the family in an ancient way: the dead receive ritual offerings of food, drink—and even cigarettes.

turning right at the next corner, circling the block and going through the same intersection again, properly this time.

Among other common-sense ways of reducing the damaging effects of everyday hostility are these suggested by Friedman: dropping acquaintances who are consistently annoying; and cultivating a habit of smiling at others, even strangers, in corridors, elevators and on the street. Even more important, Friedman advised his patients, is a sense of humor, including a not-too-serious assessment of their own imperfect selves. Among his favorite recollections was that of meeting a fellow doctor, a man who was so extraordinarily charming and relaxed that Friedman asked him how in his hectic line of work he managed not to be a Type A. The doctor smiled and replied: "A few years ago, I faced up to the truth that I always had been, and always will be, a second-rate physician. After I realized this, it was quite easy to relax."

Friedman's drastic change of life style, like his characterization of people as Type A or Type B personalities, deserves to be taken with some skepticism. The second-rate physician runs the risk of becoming a third-rate physician if he relaxes too much, and the stress sufferer who goes about the business of changing his life style too doggedly may simply be adding more stress to his life. Circling around the block may add more stress instead of teaching patience. But Friedman's regimen incorporates a principle that most physicians and psychologists would readily endorse: a change of pace or more sensible order of priorities accomplishes more than making life more bearable; for some people who are susceptible to heart attacks or ulcers, it may also mean the difference between life and death. Even a change in life style may offer little relief from stress in the great crises that inevitably strike everyone. The most powerful are those induced by family events: marriage and divorce, birth and death. These must be lived through. But their impact can be lightened by certain natural processes and social practices. The thoughtful support of friends and relatives, the free expression of joy or sadness, and the performance of prescribed ritual activities help to dissipate the extreme tensions of both pleasant and unpleasant events within the family.

The most stressful occurrence is the death of a spouse. Few people can know when such a tragedy will take place, only that it will. But if the time and place are unpredictable, the consequences are not; grief is a process that in most bereaved people follows a predictable, almost classic pattern, and a foreknowledge of that pattern can help. As many studies have shown, grief is composed of the acute arousal of alarm and fear, accompanied first by shock and numbness, then denial, a search for the lost person, anger that such a thing should happen, guilt feelings about things that were left undone or unsaid while the person was alive, depression, and finally the slow return to a more normal emotional state.

Many authorities believe that the stress of death is intensified in modern societies by a refusal to admit that in a world dedicated to happiness and eternal youth an end to life still exists. British psychiatrist Colin Murray Parkes suggested that friends and relatives often jolly the dying along not so much for the benefit of those who are suffering, but because the visitors cannot face the prospect that they too must someday die. Death, suggested British psychologist Geoffrey Gorer, has become a subject as much to be avoided in the 20th Century as sex was in the 19th —it seems pornographic. As a result, widows and widowers are avoided, almost treated as though they had a contagious disease. And grief is repressed, often with serious after effects.

Open mourning was long traditional in most societies. Generally it was part of a series of carefully prescribed rituals—ceremonial visits, special clothing, periods of withdrawal from activity—and their value in lightening the stress of death is suggested by Gorer's study of grief in modern England. He found that only a few isolated groups, such as Orthodox Jews, followed traditional mourning practices, but those that did considered them beneficial. He quotes the response of one Jewish woman he interviewed:

"It is amazing how these visits comfort you. They talk to you and start discussing the person you have lost; picture albums are brought out and everyone reminds you of little episodes in their lives. Suddenly one laughs and enjoys those memories. One's grief is lightened; it is a most healing and comforting week. Brothers and sisters who have drifted apart come together again and recall good memories. It is a comfort."

The lack of such opportunities for release may be sharply felt, as is indicated by Lynn Caine in *Widow*, a sharp-edged account of her own experiences after her husband's death. "Grief is a healing process, not a disease," she wrote, and went on to explain that it is far better if the seething and potentially damaging emotions aroused are not stoically bottled up out of some misplaced sense of dignity, but are spilled out fully and naturally in tears and even anger, and are shared with an understanding friend or relative. The bereaved individual, absorbed in the difficult work of sorting out his life and feelings, needs support and help with many practical decisions, including even the simplest chores and choices, which can seem overwhelming in the dazed state that immediately follows the events. Support is just as important after the duties of public mourning are over, when the numbness starts to wear off and the harder process of private mourning and recovery begins.

During this painful and often bewildering period, usually complicated by having to console children and relatives and take over unfamiliar and pressing financial tasks, many widows become frightened by the sheer intensity of their own emotions and need reassurance that they are not literally going mad. In her stage of "temporary insanity," as Lynn Caine described it, she made the mistake of feeling that she had to "do something"; she compounded her problems by giving up her accustomed city apartment for a new suburban life—adding the stress of moving to a new home to the stress of grief. "If I had known about stress ratings," she recalled ruefully, "it might have helped me proceed with a bit more caution."

Like many widows, she gradually found, as she worked through the stages of grief, that life could be lived on new, and in some ways better, terms. "Acceptance finally comes," she wrote, "and with it comes peace. Today I carry the scars of my bitter grief. In a way I look upon them as battle stripes, marks of my fight to attain an identity of my own." The experience changed her, she said, "Today I am someone else. I am stronger, more independent. I have more understanding, more sympathy." She believed, however, that it could have been easier for her. "If I had known the facts of grief before I had to experience them, it would not have made my grief less intense. But it would have allowed me hope. It would have given me courage. I would have known that once my grief was worked through, I would be joyful again."

The themes of hope and courage—along with faith, the sympathy and support of others, and a love of life itself—have run through stories of personal tragedy and triumph since the earliest times. For many, the ultimate weapon against stress is religious faith. Rose Kennedy—widow as well as mother of a war hero killed in action, of a President and a Senator killed by assassins, of a mentally retarded daughter and of another daughter killed in an airplane crash—has often been asked what kept her going through these stunning setbacks. In her memoirs she maintained that despite moments of pain, her life had been essentially a happy one, full of fond memories and the laughter of small events. "I have come to the conclusion," she wrote, "that the most important element in human life is faith. From faith, and through it, we come to a new understanding of ourselves and all the world about us. It puts everything into a spiritual focus . . . so that love, and joy, and happiness, along with worry, sorrow and loss, become a part of a large picture which extends far beyond time and space."

Learning how to take it

Most psychologists believe that exposure to stress increases resistance to stress; people can, in many instances, toughen themselves to withstand the blows of life. That was the aim of nine strangers who gathered in a remote section of North Carolina's mountains. There were a banker, a real-estate man, an insurance broker, a pipe fitter, a librarian, two physicians, a school teacher and photographer Fred Conrad, who photographed the group as they struggled through the rigors of an eight-day course in an Outward Bound school.

They had come to pit themselves against physical challenges so punishing that no one was sure he could get through. But when they found they could, they won for themselves a new feeling of strength, a sense of being inoculated against stress. As a former participant put it, "I know that if I want to do anything bad enough I can do it."

The first Outward Bound school was founded in 1941 in Wales by an educator, Kurt Hahn, to train young British seamen to survive shipwrecks and other wartime perils. As a name for the school, Hahn borrowed a nautical term, outward bound, that is applied to a ship leaving the safety of its port for the open sea. By the mid-1970s a worldwide network of more than 30 such schools offered wilderness adventure—sailing, mountaineering, white-water canoeing —to anyone over the age of 16 and in good health. North Carolina students got a taste of several such experiences as they learned the most important lessons Outward Bound teaches a participant: confidence in himself and concern for others.

PHOTOGRAPHED BY FRED CONRAD

Members of the Outward Bound group stop

briefly to consult their maps as they prepare to choose a campsite after a long day of backpacking through Pisgah National Forest.

Lessons to instill self-confidence

No one in the Outward Bound group was an experienced outdoorsman, and the eight days of wilderness challenge began with a minimum of preparation. The program began close to camp with practice sessions intended not only to develop physical skills but also to subject each student to psychological stress.

Mouth dry and legs shaking, each had to muster all his will power for a try at "flea hopping"—jumping across a sloping space from one perch to another *(left)*—or the grueling short climbs called bouldering *(opposite)*. But on completing the exercises, each experienced the elation of having functioned well in the face of fear.

Trembling and taut but with increasing confidence, Joffe struggles through his vertical climb. By the time he reached the top of the rock he had dispelled his self-doubt: "I climbed," he related exultantly, "just like a human monkey."

Her companions wait to catch Chris Sjogren if she falls leaping between two stumps.

Clutching his head in disbelief, Bill Joffe watches an instructor demonstrate a bouldering exercise, in which a trainee must clamber up a 16-foot rock while feeling for support with his hands and feet. Joffe recalled thinking, "I can't do that." But he did (below).

An instructor encourages Chris Sjogren to move out on a rope over the 200-foot drop called the Devil's Cellar. After it was over, Chris said, "It's hard to let go, but as soon as you do, it's okay."

Halfway across, Chris has lost her fear. "By then I was loving it. I stopped in the middle and looked down. It was so beautiful it didn't seem scary at all."

A taste of real danger

Once the Outward Bound students had learned to stand on their own blistered feet, they tackled more advanced skills, such as crossing a 200-foot-deep chasm while suspended from a rope. The student pulled himself across the gorge supported by loops that hung from a sliding metal ring; if he lost his hold on the rope and swung head downward, he had to rely on his fellows to haul him in. But none failed; each new stress brought into play reserves of strength, courage and resourcefulness none of the students had realized he possessed.

Nearing the other side, Chris grimaces with the strain of pulling herself up the steepest part of the traverse. "I was starting to feel the pull on my arm," she says. "But I never lacked confidence in the people who were securing me."

On the morning of the fifth day, the class huddles on a mountaintop, waiting for the sun to rise. Drained by repeated challenges, they are unable to summon a response to almost any stimulus. Their instructor awakened them in the pitch-black cold of morning and led them up the peak for an inspirational reading at dawn. Those who did not go back to sleep, like Chris (lower right), sit in silence. This low point midway in the course will pass, the instructors know, and group members will summon reserves of energy to meet stresses ahead.

The value of
working together

Instructor Emlyn Jones (lower right) narrowly averts disaster as he pushes his raft off a rock after plummeting down a waterfall, while his team paddles frantically toward clear water.

The sixth and seventh days of the course were devoted to white-water rafting down the foam-filled rapids of the Chattooga River. The group split into teams of three plus an instructor for each raft, and pushed off after only 30 minutes of instruction in paddling and balancing the craft. White-water excursions are the most dangerous part of this Outward Bound program, but the school considers these trips essential. During the perilous runs through the rapids, students learn a crucial lesson in group effort under stress, for if a single paddler falters, all will capsize—or as one alumnus summed it up: "The only way to survive the rapids is as a team."

After pulling their rafts to shore, the students relax in a state halfway between the exhilaration that has carried them through the trip and awe at their success.

Manhattan banker Bill Harrison slips into his own post-trip reaction: utter exhaustion.

Trying to run continuously for eight miles, Bill Joffe trails another runner, Nelson Schwab, along a hilly dirt road. Over two long stretches Joffe had to slow down to a walk; he finally finished in one hour and 33 minutes.

The triumphant end of a grueling test

Weary after their white-water trips, the group was jolted by an unexpected final test: an eight-mile foot race starting at 5:45 a.m. on the last day of the course. They were told that though they should run as fast as they could, the object was not to win the race but only to finish it.

Some later admitted that they felt competitive anyway, as though inviting even more stress in an already stressful situation. But one emotional response was felt by every student: as he crossed the finish line, he experienced a surge of self-confidence that made the race the high point of the course. Said one, "Running it was like the whole eight days in miniature. You don't necessarily want to do it again, but you feel good about having done it."

With the race—and the Outward Bound course—at an end, Joffe rocks on the school porch, enveloped in an almost visible glow of contentment. "I was so up and pleased with myself," he says, "that I was even sorry I hadn't tried harder."

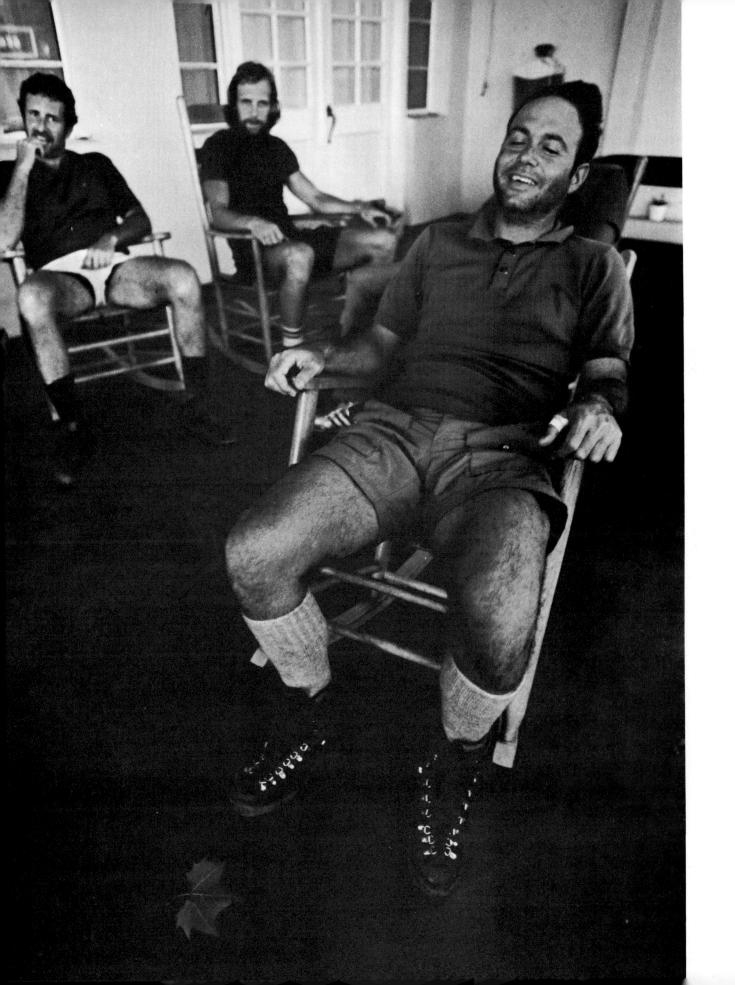

Acknowledgments

The author and editors of this book are particularly indebted to Dr. Stewart Wolf, Professor of Medicine and Physiology, Director of Marine Biomedical Institute, University of Texas, Medical Branch, Galveston. They also wish to thank the following persons and institutions: Henri Amouroux, Paris, France; Dr. Geoffrey Benjamin, Senior Lecturer in Sociology, University of Singapore, Singapore; Dr. David Blizard, Department of Neurology, New York University Medical Center, New York City; Véronique Blum, Chief Curator, B.D.I.C., Nanterre, France; Angelo Bonzanini, Professor of Labor Sociology, Rome University, Italy; George W. Brown, Professor of Sociology, Bedford College, University of London, England; Dr. Malcolm Carruthers, St. Mary's Hospital, London, England; Cécile Coutin, Curator, Musée des Deux Guerres Mondiales, Paris, France; Dr. Ruy Carlos Galanternick, Department of Psychiatry, Federal University, Rio de Janeiro, Brazil; Dr. Harold Hillman, Reader in Sociology, University of Surrey, England; Dr. Lawrence E. Hinkle Jr., Department of Medicine, The New York Hospital —Cornell Medical Center, New York City; Tomio Hirai, Faculty of Medicine, University of Tokyo, Japan; Dr. J. L. Kearns, London, England; Dr. Samuel Z. Klausner, Director, Center for Research on the Acts of Man, Philadelphia, Pennsylvania; Dr. Arthur Kleinman, Department of Psychiatry, Massachusetts General Hospital, Boston; Dr. Pierre Lacombe, Paris, France; Dr. Malcolm Lader, Institute of Psychiatry, London, England; Gastone Marri, Rome, Italy; Cesare Musatti, Professor Emeritus, Milan University, Italy; Raffaele Nisiti, Director, Institute of Psychology, Consiglio Nazionale Delle Ricerche, Rome, Italy; Franco Novara, Director, Center of Psychology, Olivetti, Ivrea, Italy; Alain Rollet, Press Attaché, Ministry of Health, Paris, France; François Wittmann, Paris, France.

Bibliography

Barton, Allen H., *Communities in Disaster: A Sociological Analysis of Collective Stress Situations*. Doubleday & Co., 1970.

Basowits, Harold, Harold Persky, Sheldon J. Korchin and Roy G. Grinker, *Anxiety and Stress*. McGraw-Hill Book Co., Inc., 1955.

Bourne, Peter G., *The Psychology and Physiology of Stress*. Academic Press, 1969.

Caine, Lynn, *Widow*. William Morrow & Co., 1974.

Cannon, Walter B., *Bodily Changes in Pain, Hunger, Fear and Rage*. Charles T. Branford Co., 1953.

Caplan, Gerald, *Principles of Preventive Psychiatry*. Basic Books, Inc., 1964.

Carruthers, Malcolm, *The Western Way of Death*. Davis-Poynter, Ltd., 1974.

Dank, Milton, *The French Against the French*. J. B. Lippincott Co., 1974.

Dodge, David L., and Walter T. Martin, *Social Stress and Chronic Illness: Mortality Patterns in Industrial Society*. University of Notre Dame Press, 1970.

Dohrenwend, Barbara Snell and Bruce P., eds., *Stressful Life Events: Their Nature and Effects*. John Wiley & Sons, 1974.

Dubos, René Jules, *Man Adapting*. Yale University Press, 1965.

Freedman, Jonathan L., *Crowding and Behavior*. Viking Press, Inc., 1975.

Friedman, Arnold P., and Shervert H. Frazier Jr., *The Headache Book*. Dodd, Mead & Co., 1973.

Friedman, Meyer, and Ray H. Rosenman, *Type A Behavior and Your Heart*. Alfred A. Knopf, 1974.

Galton, Lawrence, *The Silent Disease: Hypertension*. New American Library, 1973.

Glass, David C., and Jerome E. Singer, *Urban Stress: Experiments on Noise and Social Stressors*. Academic Press, 1972.

Grinker, Roy R., and John P. Spiegel, *Men Under Stress*. The Blakiston Co., 1945.

Gunderson, E. K. Eric, and Richard H. Rahe, eds., *Life Stress and Illness*. Charles C. Thomas, Publisher, 1974.

Hall, Edward T., *The Hidden Dimension*. Doubleday & Co., Inc., 1966.

Helmer, John, and Neil A. Eddington, eds., *Urbanman: The Psychology of Urban Survival*. The Free Press, 1973.

Ittelson, William H., Harold M. Proshansky, Leanne G. Rivlin, Gary H. Winkel, *An Introduction to Environmental Psychology*. Holt, Rinehart and Winston, Inc., 1974.

Janis, Irving L.:
Air War and Emotional Stress. McGraw-Hill Book Co., Inc., 1951.
Psychological Stress. John Wiley & Sons, 1958.

Jonas, Gerald, *Visceral Learning: Toward a Science of Self-Control*. Cornerstone Library, 1973.

Kiev, Ari, *A Strategy for Handling Executive Stress*. Nelson-Hall, 1974.

Klausner, Samuel Z., ed., *Why Man Takes Chances: Studies in Stress-Seeking*. Doubleday & Co., Inc., 1968.

Koestler, Arthur, *The Act of Creation*. The Macmillan Co., 1967.

Langner, Thomas S., and Stanley T. Michael, *Life Stress and Mental Health*. The Free Press, 1963.

Lazarus, R. S., *Psychological Stress & Coping Process*. McGraw-Hill Book Co., 1966.

Levi, Lennart, ed.:
Emotions: Their Parameters and Measurement. Raven Press, Publishers, 1975.
Society, Stress, and Disease. Oxford University Press, 1971.
Stress and Distress in Response to Psychosocial Stimuli. Pergamon Press, 1972.

Lewis, Howard R., and Martha E., *Psychosomatics: How Your Emotions Can Damage Your Health*. Pinnacle Books, 1975.

Marshall, S. L. A.:
Men against Fire. William Morrow & Co., 1955.
The Soldier's Load and the Mobility of a Nation. The Marine Corps Associa-

tion, 1965.

McLean, Alan, *Occupational Stress.* Charles C. Thomas, Publisher, 1974.

McQuade, Walter, and Ann Aikman, *Stress.* E. P. Dutton & Co., Inc., 1974.

Menninger, Karl, Martin Mayman and Paul Pruyser, *Vital Balance: The Life Process in Mental Health and Illness.* Viking Press, Inc., 1963.

Merton, Robert K., and Robert A. Nisbet, eds., *Contemporary Social Problems.* Harcourt, Brace & World, Inc., 1961.

Miller, Benjamin F., and Lawrence Galton, *Freedom from Heart Attacks.* Simon and Schuster, 1972.

National Institute of Mental Health, *The Mental Health of Urban America.* Health Services and Mental Health Administration of U.S. Department of Health, Education, and Welfare, April 1969.

Parkes, Colin Murray, *Bereavement: Studies of Grief in Adult Life.* Penguin Books, 1975.

Piddington, Ralph, *The Psychology of Laughter.* Gamut Press, Inc., 1963.

Proshansky, Harold M., William H. Ittelson and Leanne G. Rivlin, *Environmental Psychology: Man and His Physical Setting.* Holt, Rinehart and Winston, Inc., 1970.

Selye, Hans:
Stress without Distress. J. B. Lippincott Co., 1974.
The Stress of Life. McGraw-Hill Book Co., Inc., 1956.

Silverman, Samuel:
How Will You Feel Tomorrow? New Ways to Predict Illness. Stein and Day, Publishers, 1973.
Psychologic Cues in Forecasting Physical Illness. Appleton-Century-

Crofts, 1970.

Simeons, A. T. W., *Man's Presumptuous Brain.* E. P. Dutton & Co., Inc., 1960.

Slater, Philip, *The Pursuit of Loneliness: American Culture at the Breaking Point.* Beacon Press, 1970.

Sommer, Robert, *Personal Space: The Behavioral Basis of Design.* Prentice-Hall, Inc., 1969.

Stearns, Frederic R., *Laughing: Physiology, Pathophysiology, Psychology, Pathopsychology and Development.* Charles C. Thomas, Publisher, 1972.

Stellman, Jeanne M., and Susan M. Daum, *Work Is Dangerous to Your Health.* Vintage Books, 1973.

Wallace, Robert Keith, *The Physiological Effects of Transcendental Meditation.* Herbert Herz Co., Inc., 1971.

Wolff, Harold G., *Stress and Disease,* 2nd ed. Charles C. Thomas, Publisher, 1968.

Picture Credits

The sources for the illustrations in this book are shown below. Credits from left to right are separated by semicolons, from top to bottom by dashes.

Cover—Ernst Haas. 6—Ernst Haas, photographed at Rockaways' Playland, Rockaway Beach, N.Y. 10—Eddie Adams from TIME-LIFE Picture Agency. 12—Ewing Galloway except middle, Erik Ruby, taken from *The Human Figure* published by Van Nostrand Reinhold Co. 14—John Olson from TIME-LIFE Picture Agency. 16—Marvin E. Newman. 17—Drawing by Nicholas Fasciano, adapted from The Ciba Collection of Medical Illustrations by Frank H. Netter, M.D. 20, 21—Leonard Freed from Magnum. 22—*Hackensack Record.* 24—Jim Mahan from TIME-LIFE Picture Agency. 26, 27—Seymour Epstein. 30, 31—George Silk from TIME-LIFE Picture Agency. 32, 33—Walter Iooss Jr. for SPORTS ILLUSTRATED; Francisco Hidalgo. 34, 35—Alfred Eisenstaedt from TIME-LIFE Picture Agency. 36, 37—Henri Cartier-Bresson from Magnum; Dennis Connor for UPI. 38, 39—Constantine Manos from Magnum. 40—Matthew Klein. 44, 45—Jim Marshall © 1975. 47—Nilo

Olin of the National Institute of Mental Health. 48—David Hurn from Magnum. 50—TIME-LIFE Picture Agency. 52, 53—Dufoto; Press Association—Paris Match. 54—Serge de Sazo from Rapho/Photo Researchers. 56, 57—Sankei Shimbun from TIME-LIFE Picture Agency. 60, 61—Ken Kay. 64—Shelly Rusten. 66—John Launois from Black Star. 68 through 79—Gilles Peress from Magnum. 80, 84—New York *Daily News.* 87—Paul Schutzer from TIME-LIFE Picture Agency. 89—Ian Berry from Magnum. 91—Constantine Manos from Magnum, taken from *A Greek Portfolio;* scale from *Journal of Psychosomatic Research,* 1967. 94, 95—Ilhan Demirel from Sipa-Press. 97—Hans H. Pinn from TIME-LIFE Picture Agency. 98—W. Eugene Smith © 1973 ICP/The Concerned Photographer. 102, 103—Tran Dai Minh for UPI. 106, 107—Bundesarchiv, Koblenz, West Germany. 108, 109—Gene Laurents; Roger Schall; Robert Doisneau from Rapho/Photo Researchers—Wide World. 110, 111—Ralph Morse from TIME-LIFE Picture Agency; Bob Landry from TIME-LIFE Picture Agency—Courtesy Archives R. Galeyrand, taken from *Ceux du D.A.F.* by André Delapierre; Courtesy Etablissement Cinématographique des Armées. 112—Collec-

tion S.A.F.A.R.A., Cabinet des Estampes, Bibliothèque Nationale, Paris—Courtesy Centre de Documentation Juive Contemporaine, Paris. 113—Roger Schall—Ullstein Bilderdienst, West Berlin. 114, 115—Robert Doisneau from Rapho/Photo Researchers—Etablissement Cinématographique des Armées; Collection Viollet—Pierre Boulat. 116, 117—Bob Landry from TIME-LIFE Picture Agency; Frank Scherschel from TIME-LIFE Picture Agency. 118—Constantine Manos from Magnum. 121—John Dominis from TIME-LIFE Picture Agency. 122—Leonard Freed from Magnum. 124—Velio Cioni from TIME-LIFE Picture Agency—Ted Needham for the *San Francisco Examiner.* 125—Sven Simon. 129—Henri Cartier-Bresson from Magnum. 133—Lennart Nilsson from TIME-LIFE Picture Agency. 135, 136, 137—Drawings by Robert Osborn. 140—George Haling. 144—Gilles Peress from Magnum. 146—Paul Fusco from Magnum. 150—Stan Wayman from TIME-LIFE Picture Agency. 153—Howard Sochurek from TIME-LIFE Picture Agency. 154, 155—Malcolm S. Kirk—Carl Roodman from Photo Researchers; Klaus Paysan; John Launois from Black Star. 156—Albert Moldvay. 160 through 171—Fred R. Conrad.

Printed in U.S.A.